100
American Women
Who Changed the World

Publications International, Ltd.

Table of Contents

Introduction

"Well-behaved women seldom make history."

This quote, so often found on coffee mugs, t-shirts, and bumper stickers, has been attributed to everyone from Marilyn Monroe to Anne Boleyn. But the phrase actually originated in a 1976 paper by University of New Hampshire history student Laurel Thatcher Ulrich—well after Boleyn and Monroe's eras. Ulrich's paper explored the "well-behaved" women in 17th and 18th century New England, who quietly went about their lives and duties, barely ever attracting notice or securing a place in history books— unlike their more outspoken male counterparts.

It's not that these women did nothing of consequence; they were vitally important members of their society. They were midwives, healers, farmers, travelers, and mothers. Some were even the main breadwinners of their families, selling goods or livestock and earning more income than their husbands. But their modest, simple lives garnered little mention in historical records.

Interestingly, Ulrich's college paper, which sought to bring recognition to women long forgotten, ended up landing her in the history books, as well—even though the quote is often misattributed. She later went on to win a Pulitzer Prize and is currently a renowned history professor at Harvard University. And the quote she made famous has become a bit of a rallying cry for women's rights advocates, who have embraced the idea of "misbehaving" in their efforts to be seen and heard.

Fortunately, the Puritan standards of "misbehavior" have evolved over time, as more and more women have lived their lives with determination and tenacity, recognizing that their contributions to society are not limited by outdated—and often male-dominated—standards. These women encompass all walks of life, all races, all professions, all personalities; they serve as examples and inspiration not only for those of us in the present, but for future generations, as well.

The names in this book are an example of the diverse and distinct pioneers who have paved the way for women everywhere. We'll read about entertainers like Kathryn Bigelow, the first woman to win an Oscar for Best Director, and artists like architect Maya Lin, who designed the Vietnam Veteran's Memorial. We'll see how six-year-old Ruby Bridges bravely became the first African-American child to desegregate an all-white school, and how Sally Ride rocketed into history books with her trip to space. We'll read about Betty Friedan's "feminine mystique," and learn why Abigail Adams was called "Mrs. President." We'll even discover Lady Gaga's real name and find out how she came about her unusual moniker.

And of course, no list of great American women would be complete without some of the most recognizable names in our country's history: Rosa Parks, Hillary Clinton, Sandra Day O'Connor, Coretta Scott King, and so many more who have made a lasting impression on America's history.

It is said that behind every great man there is a great woman; perhaps the same can be said for great countries: America would not be the country it is today without the women who helped to shape it with their ideas, their intelligence, their self-confidence, and their resolve. Misbehaved or not, these women made history.

Angelina Jolie

Angelina Jolie Voight was born into an acting family on June 4, 1975. Her father, Jon Voight, and mother, Marcheline Bertrand, were both actors, and Jolie's very first acting role was alongside her father in 1982's *Lookin' to Get Out*. Surprisingly, Jolie—who frequently appears on lists of the "most beautiful women in the world"—was frequently teased in the halls of Beverly Hills High School, due to her thin, awkward appearance and modest attire, which stood out from her richer classmates' clothing.

But it's safe to say that Jolie had the last laugh. After starring in a handful of mostly forgettable films, she found her big break in 1998 when she portrayed model Gia Carangi in the HBO film *Gia*. Jolie won a Golden Globe award and was nominated for an Emmy for her performance, and soon, her career skyrocketed. Her impressive turn in 1999's *Girl, Interrupted* earned her an Academy Award for Best Supporting Actress, and 2001's *Lara Croft: Tomb Raider* made her an international superstar.

Besides her lengthy list of hit films—including *Mr. & Mrs. Smith, Salt,* and *Maleficent*—Jolie is also a prolific producer and director, and a Goodwill Ambassador for the United Nations High Commissioner for Refugees. She frequently donates out of her own pocket to charities close to her heart, especially organizations aimed at providing education to children worldwide, ending child poverty, and providing health services to children in impoverished countries.

(Above) Jolie poses on the red carpet before a film screening at the Cannes Film Festival.

(Bottom right) Angelina Jolie visits Pakistan to meet with women who were affected by a flood.

Julia Child

Although we associate the name Julia Child with cooking, Child—who was born Julia Carolyn McWilliams on August 15, 1912, in Pasadena, California—was not a natural talent. In fact, when she was growing up, Child's family employed a cook, making the need for chef skills obsolete.

During World War II, Child joined the Office of Strategic Services (the predecessor of today's CIA) as a typist, but soon moved up in the ranks and worked at several posts around the world. It was when she was posted to Kunming, China, that she met fellow OSS employee Paul Cushing Child. The pair married on September 1, 1946, and in 1948 they moved to Paris.

Paul was a fan of the French cuisine they enjoyed in their adopted city, and Child set out to learn as much as she could about the cooking style. She attended the Le Cordon Bleu cooking school and joined an exclusive women's cooking club called *Le Cercle des Gourmettes*, where she met Simone Beck and Louisette Bertholle. The three women collaborated on a French cookbook specifically written for Americans. The book, *Mastering the Art of French Cooking*, became an instant best seller.

The success of the book led to Child's first cooking show, *The French Chef*, which debuted on February 11, 1963. The show immediately appealed to American housewives, who considered Child authentic and approachable. The writer and TV chef's career spanned four decades, and included more than two dozen cooking shows and cookbooks, which still appeal to home chefs today.

Mary Tyler Moore

Born on December 29, 1936, in Brooklyn, New York, Mary Tyler Moore knew by the time she was a teenager that she wanted to be a performer. She danced and acted in high school, landing her first paying job at the age of 17 when she played the part of "Happy Hotpoint," an elf who danced in commercials for Hotpoint appliances.

Her dancer's legs helped her break into television, where her first role was that of Sam, a secretary on the drama *Richard Diamond, Private Detective*. Moore's voice was heard, but her mysterious character was only represented by her shapely legs. Her face was never seen.

After guest appearances on shows like *77 Sunset Strip* and *Hawaiian Eye*, Moore became a household name when she was cast as the charming, energetic Laura Petrie on *The Dick Van Dyke Show*. The actress showed off a talent for comedy—and made capri pants a fashion statement—and won two Emmys for her performance.

When the show ended in 1966, Moore moved on to movies and musicals, thinking her television popularity had probably hit its peak. She appeared in the musicals *Thoroughly Modern Millie* opposite Julie Andrews, and *Change of Habit* with Elvis Presley, as well as movie comedies like *Don't Just Stand There*. But in 1970, Moore and her then-husband, Grant Tinker, pitched a sitcom to CBS with Moore playing the central character. *The Mary Tyler Moore Show* debuted in September of 1970, and was an immediate hit.

(Left) Mary Tyler Moore's star on the Hollywood Boulevard Walk of Fame

(Below) A statue of Mary Richards, Mary Tyler Moore's television persona, outside Macy's Store in Minneapolis

Moore's show, in which her main character was a single, professional career woman living alone in Minneapolis, became a cultural phenomenon. Whereas other shows of the era centered around men, with women playing roles of housewives or secretaries, *The Mary Tyler Moore Show* echoed the changing roles of women in the workplace. Moore won three Emmys for the sitcom, which ran until 1977.

The actress went on to appear in many shows and movies—most notably in 1980's *Ordinary People*, for which she received an Oscar nomination—but she will always be fondly remembered as the iconic Mary Richards. A statue of her character tossing her hat in the air—as was shown in the opening of every episode—was unveiled in downtown Minneapolis in 2002.

Mary Pickford

Long before Julia Roberts or Jennifer Lawrence captured the hearts of audiences, another actress took the title of "America's Sweetheart": Mary Pickford. Pickford was born Gladys Louise Smith on April 8, 1892, in Toronto, Ontario, Canada. Pickford came from an acting family, who toured the United States by rail searching for acting jobs.

By the early 1900s, silent films were becoming increasingly popular in the country, and Pickford auditioned for New York director D.W. Griffith, who was immediately taken with the ingénue. Pickford appeared in more than 40 of Griffith's films in 1909, and then followed him to California in 1910.

Although actors were not named in the credits of Griffith's films, audiences were immediately drawn to "The Girl with the Golden Curls." She appeared in hits like *Poor Little Rich Girl* and *Polyanna*, and worked behind the scenes as a producer, as well. In 1919, along with Griffith, Charlie Chaplin, and Douglas Fairbanks Sr., Pickford founded the United Artists film company.

In 1929, Pickford stared in her first talking picture, *Coquette*, for which she won an Oscar for Best Actress; unfortunately, her roles in talking films were never as popular as her silent films, and she made her last movie in 1933. But Pickford's savvy business sense made her a pioneer for women in the early days of film, and she remained on the board of directors of United Artists for many years.

(Top left) Mary Pickford in the film The Little Princess *(1917)*

(Bottom left) Pickford in the film Rebecca of Sunnybrook Farm *(1917)*

Cindy Sherman

Cindy Sherman was born in Glen Ridge, New Jersey, on January 19, 1954. After high school, she attended Buffalo State College where she studied visual arts. Although she began as a painter, she soon decided photography gave her more freedom to express herself. Sherman began dressing in outfits she bought at thrift stores and photographing herself as different characters.

In 1977, this process morphed into her *Untitled Film Stills* series, which is her best-known body of work. The collection of 69 black and white photographs depicts Sherman in different costumes and locations, in the style of film noir. The photos challenged the cultural stereotypes of women in film, and she created her characters to be rebellious women who eschewed the norms of marriage and family.

In the '80s and '90s, Sherman began experimenting with color photography, sometimes using posed mannequins for models. By the 2000s, Sherman was able to use digital photography to manipulate subjects and backgrounds, always sticking with her theme of challenging society's view of women.

Sherman's work has been exhibited around the world, from the San Francisco Museum of Modern Art to the Serpentine Gallery in London. In 1995, the Museum of Modern Art in New York purchased her *Untitled Film Stills* series for an estimated $1 million.

Cindy Sherman attends the Time 100 *Gala (left) and the Planned Parenthood 100 Anniversary Gala (right).*

Mia Farrow

Perhaps best known for her role as Rosemary in the unsettling 1968 film *Rosemary's Baby*, Mia Farrow is much more than just an actress. Born Maria de Lourdes Villiers Farrow on February 9, 1945, in Los Angeles, California, Farrow grew up in Beverly Hills, perhaps destined to take part in the entertainment industry. She first worked as a model before breaking into acting, with her first popular role being Allison MacKenzie on the soap opera *Peyton Place*.

Farrow's peformance in *Rosemary's Baby* earned her a Golden Globe Award. Her classical performance was praised around the world, and in the 1970s, Farrow became the first American actress invited to join to Royal Shakespeare Company in London. Farrow's many film appearances include *The Great Gatsby, Peter Pan,* and *A Wedding*, and throughout the 1980s and 90s, she starred in more than a dozen of director— and former-husband—Woody Allen's films.

(Above) Mia Farrow visits a school as a UNICEF Goodwill Ambassador.

While Farrow has continued to act, her true passion began in 2000, when she became a UNICEF Goodwill Ambassador. Her work has led her campaign for human rights in Africa, and she has traveled extensively throughout the continent to advocate for children, including to the Sudan, Rwanda, Sierra Leone, and the Central African Republic. She has participated in several documentaries bringing awareness to the plight of children in war-torn countries around the world.

Farrow's efforts and work for humanitarian causes led *Time* magazine to name her one of the most influential people in the world in 2008.

Beyoncé Knowles

(Above) Kelly Rowland, Michelle Williams, and Beyoncé perform as Destiny's Child in 2005 in New York City.

Known as simply "Beyoncé" and "Queen Bey" by her loyal fans, Beyoncé Giselle Knowles was born on September 4, 1981, in Houston, Texas. She loved music and performing from an early age, and at only eight years old was part of a singing group called Girl's Tyme that competed on the show *Star Search*. Although the group failed to win, they continued to perform together, eventually changing their name to Destiny's Child.

In 1998, Destiny's Child released their first album, but it was their multi-platinum second album, *The Writing's on the Wall*, that put the group—and especially Beyoncé—on the map in 1999. In 2003, the singer released her first solo album, *Dangerously in Love*, which featured her first number-one single, "Crazy in Love." Beyoncé also tried her hand at acting, appearing in several films, including *The Fighting Temptations*, *The Pink Panther*, and *Dreamgirls*.

In 2008, Beyoncé married rapper and hip-hop artist Jay-Z, with former Destiny's Child members Kelly Rowland and Michelle Williams in attendance at the ceremony. In the decade since, Beyoncé's career has hit many high notes: She performed for President Barack Obama and First Lady Michelle Obama at the inaugural ball, started a clothing line called House of Dereon, launched her own perfume, became a spokesperson for brands like L'Oreal and Tommy Hilfiger, and performed at two Super Bowls.

But perhaps Beyoncé's happiest achievements are her children with Jay-Z—daughter, Blue Ivy, and twins Rumi and Sir. In fact, the singer's Instagram announcement on February 1, 2017, confirming her twin pregnancy broke the world record for the most-liked image on the website.

There's no doubt that Beyoncé is one of the most influential entertainers of our time, and the singer, actress, entrepreneur, and mother keeps proving it. She just may be—as *The New Yorker* music critic Jody Rosen once said—"the most important and compelling popular musician of the twenty-first century."

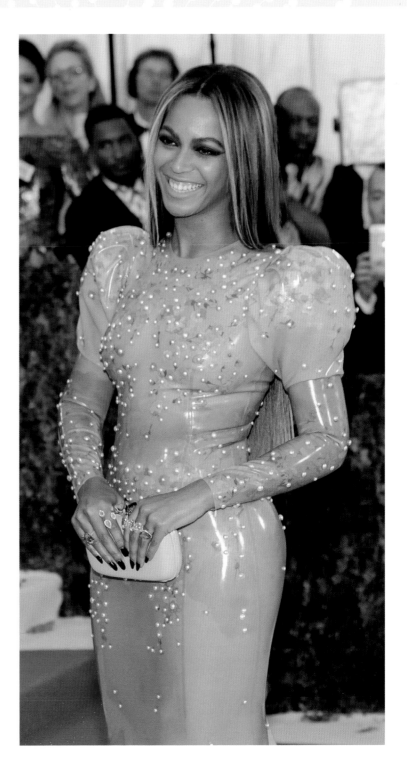

Hattie McDaniel

Hattie McDaniel was born on June 10, 1895, in Wichita, Kansas. The youngest of 13 children born to former slaves, McDaniel—along with her brother Sam and sister Etta—was a performer from a young age, creating family minstrel shows with her siblings. McDaniel loved to sing, and in the 1920s she began a radio career, becoming the first African-American woman to sing on the radio in the U.S.

After three of her siblings moved to Los Angeles, McDaniel joined them in 1931. Working as a cook and a maid, she persistently pursued her love of performing, eventually landing her first film role in 1932's *The Golden West*. Throughout the 1930s, McDaniel worked steadily in movies, appearing in films like *China Seas* with Clark Gable, *Murder by Television* with Bela Lugosi, and the musical *Show Boat*. She befriended some of the most popular stars of the time, hobnobbing with the likes of Joan Crawford, Bette Davis, and Ronald Reagan.

But it was her role as Mammy in 1939's *Gone with the Wind* that cemented McDaniel's place as a Hollywood superstar. She won the Academy Award for Best Supporting Actress, becoming the first black American to be nominated and win an Oscar.

In total, McDaniel appeared in more than 300 films, making her a prolific performer by any measure. She was honored with two stars on the Hollywood Walk of Fame—one for her radio work, and one for her film work.

(Top left) Hattie McDaniel on the radio program Beluah

(Bottom left) A headshot of McDaniel

Ella Fitzgerald

Born in Newport News, Virginia, on April 25, 1917, Ella Fitzgerald loved to sing and dance from her earliest years. Raised by her mother and stepfather, the family moved from Virginia to Yonkers, New York, in the early 1920s. Fitzgerald's mother often brought home jazz records, and young Ella was entranced by the sounds of Louis Armstrong, Bing Crosby, and the Boswell Sisters.

Although a good student, Fitzgerald's studies faltered after her mother was killed in a car accident. Despondent, Fitzgerald dropped out of school, left home, and survived by singing for money on the streets of Harlem. But in 1934, her life changed when she won first prize in a singing contest at New York's famed Apollo Theater. She went on to join the Chick Webb orchestra, and began recording songs. Her first major hit, "A-Tisket, A-Tasket" made her a popular household name.

In 1942, she began soloing, and she toured internationally with artists like Benny Goodman, Duke Ellington, and Dizzy Gillespie. But the highpoint of her career came in the late '50s and early '60s, when she recorded nearly 250 songs by composers such as George Gershwin and Cole Porter. Fitzgerald—who won a total of 14 Grammy Awards in her lifetime—performed each song with such masterful vocal interpretation that she earned the enduring nicknames "The First Lady of Song" and "Queen of Jazz."

(Right) A photo of Ella Fitzgerald from 1946

Ellen DeGeneres

Born on January 26, 1958, in Metairie, Louisiana, Ellen DeGeneres surprisingly was not considered the funny member of the family. That distinction went to her older brother, Vance, an actor and comedian who appeared on the satire news program *The Daily Show* from 1999 to 2001. Growing up, DeGeneres dreamed of becoming a veterinarian, but later majored in communication studies at the University of New Orleans. After only one semester, DeGeneres left college and began working odd jobs—doing clerical work, waiting tables, painting houses, and tending bar.

At the age of 23, DeGeneres decided to try her hand at comedy,

(Below left) Ellen DeGeneres and her wife, Portia de Rossi, attend the 41st Annual People's Choice Awards in 2015.

(Below right) DeGeneres dances with First Lady Michelle Obama on The Ellen DeGeneres Show.

doing stand-up at Clyde's Comedy Club in New Orleans. Her routine was a huge hit, and before long she was the club's emcee. She began touring nationally, and when Jay Leno happened to catch her act at the Improv in Hollywood, she was invited to appear on *The Tonight Show Starring Johnny Carson*. After her routine, Carson invited her to sit next to him—although this seemed like a small gesture, it was widely known to those in the entertainment industry that this was Carson's signal that he believed his guest to be especially talented. DeGeneres was the first female comic to be invited to sit next to Carson in this place of honor.

Her success on *The Tonight Show* led to a transition from stand-up comedy to sitcom star, and her show *Ellen* debuted in 1994. It was on this show in 1997 that her character—and DeGeneres herself—came out as gay. *Ellen* became the first primetime show with an openly gay character, and is still considered to have a groundbreaking place in television history.

Today, DeGeneres is best known for her popular, Emmy-winning talk show, *The Ellen DeGeneres Show*, as well as for the voice of Dory in the Pixar films *Finding Nemo* and *Finding Dory*. She has been married to actress Portia de Rossi—who legally changed her name to Portia Lee James DeGeneres—since 2008.

Oprah Winfrey

Born to a teen mother in Kosciusko, Mississippi, in 1954, Oprah Winfrey was raised by her grandmother in extreme poverty. Despite her living conditions, Winfrey's grandmother taught her to read at a young age. When she was six, Winfrey moved to Milwaukee to live with her mother and half-sister, and was then sent to live with her father in Nashville, as her mother could not support both children.

After returning to Milwaukee, Winfrey was able to attend an affluent high school, but was often bullied for her poverty. After stealing money from her mother in an attempt to fit in with her classmates, she was once again sent to live in Nashville with her father. While in Nashville, she focused on her education and joined the high school speech team, which led to a full scholarship at Tennessee State University.

During college, Winfrey was hired by a local black radio station to cover the news. After school, she continued working at radio stations and television stations all around the country. In 1983, she took a job at a low-rated morning talk show in Chicago. However, after just a few months, the ratings skyrocketed, and she was offered a deal for *The Oprah Winfrey Show* in 1986. Eventually, her show became the number one daytime talk show in America.

The Oprah Winfrey Show expanded from being mainly a tabloid talk show to covering heavier topics like politics, diseases, social issues, and spirituality. Winfrey was also known to talk about personal, intimate details

(Left) Winfrey attends the premiere of **A Wrinkle in Time.**

of her own life on her show, gaining a loyal fan following in the process. The show aired until May of 2011.

In addition to her talk show, Winfrey co-founded the *Oxygen* television network and founded Harpo Productions and her own television channel, *OWN: Oprah Winfrey Network*. She has co-authored five books and co-starred in several films including *The Color Purple, A Wrinkle in Time*, and *The Princess and the Frog*.

Winfrey is often considered one of the world's most powerful women and most influential African Americans by major news sources. She has appeared in *TIME's* most influential people list ten times. She is also known for her generous charitable contributions and humanitarianism, and she became a recipient of the Presidential Medal of Freedom in 2013. In 2018, Winfrey was awarded the Golden Globes' Cecil B. DeMille Award, for life-time achievement, where her acceptance speech became an iconic cry for an end to a culture of oppressive and abusive men.

(Below left) President Barack Obama presents Winfrey with the Presidential Medal of Freedom.

(Below right) Winfrey at the 75th Golden Globes Press Room

Maya Lin

The daughter of Chinese immigrants, Maya Lin was born in Athens, Ohio, on October 5, 1959. The studious Lin loved school, art, and caring for the environment, even as a child. While studying architecture at Yale University in 1981, she entered a public competition to design the Vietnam Veterans Memorial. Lin incorporated her love of the environment into her design, creating a simple memorial that rises from the earth around it.

Surprisingly, the inexperienced 21-year-old architect beat out 1,421 other hopefuls, submitting the winning entry. But her success was not without controversy: Some felt the design was too boring and unconventional, unbefitting of a war memorial. Others objected to Lin's Asian heritage, with Lin herself believing she would not have won had the entries not been anonymously submitted by each artist by number.

Today, the Vietnam Veterans Memorial is the most visited war memorial in the country, greeting close to 6 million visitors every year. Lin now operates her own studio in New York City, and in 2016 was awarded the Presidential Medal of Freedom—the highest civilian award in the United States.

(Below) The Vietnam Veterans Memorial in Washington, D.C. honors those who served in, died in, or went missing in action during the Vietnam War.

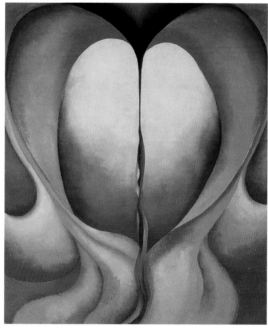
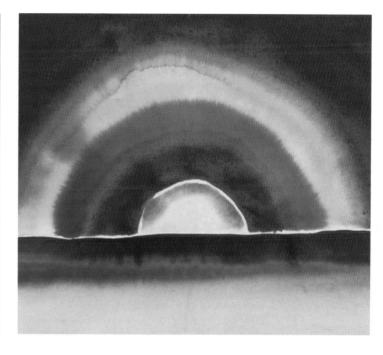

Georgia O'Keeffe

(Above) Paintings (left to right): Red Canna, 1919; Series 1, No. 8, 1919; Sunrise, 1916

Born in a farmhouse in Sun Prairie, Wisconsin, on November 15, 1887, Georgia O'Keeffe knew by the age of age of 10 that she wanted to be an artist. She studied art throughout high school, and after graduation she attended the Art Institute of Chicago and the Art Students League in New York City.

After her family fell on hard times, O'Keeffe was unable to continue her studies, but was able to find work as a commercial artist, and then taught art in public schools and colleges. While teaching at Columbia College in Columbia, South Carolina, O'Keeffe began a series of charcoal drawings, which she mailed to her friend, Anita Pollitzer.

Pollitzer, in turn, showed the drawings to influential art dealer Alfred Stieglitz, who exhibited her work at his gallery, 291.

O'Keeffe and Stieglitz continued to work together, and eventually married. With Stieglitz promoting her work, O'Keeffe dove into her artwork, becoming known especially for her paintings of flowers, skyscrapers, animal skulls, and New Mexico landscapes. By the 1920s, she was the highest paid American woman artist, displaying a distinctive style that was viewed as groundbreaking in the art world.

O'Keeffe was awarded the Presidential Medal of Freedom in 1977, and the National Medal of Arts in 1985.

Laverne Cox

Laverne Cox and her identical twin brother, M Lamar, were raised by a single mother and grandmother in Mobile, Alabama. At the young age of 11, a depressed Cox attempted suicide after fighting attractions to male classmates; but her love of dance and performance gave her hopes and dreams for the future, and she continued to endure.

Soon after her suicide attempt, Cox earned a scholarship to the Alabama School of Fine Arts—a boarding school in Birmingham, Alabama. While there, she studied classical ballet and then accepted a scholarship to Indiana University at Bloomington, where she continued to dance. She later transferred to Marymount Manhattan College and graduated with a bachelor of fine arts degree in dance. It was at Marymount where she first started to embrace acting. She appeared in several plays for the Marymount theater department, a few student films, and several off-Broadway productions.

But ironically, Cox's big break would come from just being herself. In 2009, she was asked to be on VH1's *I Want to Work for Diddy*. Although she only appeared in two episodes, producers were so impressed with her that they asked her for show ideas. This led to Cox's own reality show, *TRANSform Me*, and Cox became the first African-American transgender person to produce and star in her own show.

2013 would bring another first: This was the year Cox first

appeared on the Netflix hit series *Orange is the New Black*, starring as Sophia Burset, a transgender woman sent to prison for credit card fraud. Cox's brother, M Lamar, also appeared on the show as Marcus, the pre-transitioning Sophia. The show marks the first time an African-American transgender woman was given a leading role on a mainstream scripted television series, and Cox earned two Emmy nominations for her performance.

Cox continues to act, produce, and write, using her platform to fight for equality, spread awareness, and advocate for the transgender community.

(Left) Cox at the 2016 Primetime Emmy Awards

(Below) Cox attends the Gay Pride parade in Manhattan in 2014.

Lucille Ball

Before Oprah, Cher, or Madonna made the single-name moniker popular, there was Lucille Desiree Ball—known to millions around the world as simply "Lucy." The actress was born on August 6, 1911, in Jamestown, New York. After her father died of typhoid fever when she was only three years old, Lucy, her mother, and her younger brother, Frederick, moved to nearby Celoron to live with her maternal grandparents. Both her mother and grandparents encouraged her to participate in school plays and took her to the theater, sparking an interest in the craft.

In 1926, Lucy enrolled in the John Murray Anderson/Robert Milton School of Theater and Dance in New York City, where actress Bette Davis was a classmate. But unlike Davis, who excelled at school, Lucy was considered a poor student and a dismal failure. Her mother even received a letter from the faculty saying her daughter could never succeed in the entertainment industry and it was a waste of money to continue paying for the school. Undeterred by the criticism, Lucy vowed to prove her instructors wrong. But it would take nearly two more decades before the actress would find true fame.

Throughout the 1930s, Lucy had some moderate success, appearing in small parts in films and on Broadway, and landing a job as the Chesterfield cigarette girl. During this time, she worked with comic legends like the Three Stooges, the Marx Brothers, Laurel and Hardy, and Buster Keaton. The lessons she

(Above) A photo of Lucille Ball from an issue of Yank, the Army Weekly, *a U.S. Army magazine*

learned from these comedy masters would shape the rest of her career.

In 1940, Lucy met Cuban bandleader Desi Arnaz on the set of the film *Too Many Girls*. The pair quickly eloped, but the union was plagued with difficulties from the start, with work schedules constantly keeping them apart. In an effort to save their marriage and spend more time together, Lucy and Desi developed a television pilot and formed a production company, Desilu Productions. The television pilot, of course, was *I Love Lucy*, which ultimately ran for six seasons and won five Emmy Awards. Lucy's zany housewife persona was beloved by Americans, and *I Love Lucy* became the first television show in history to be broadcast to more than ten million homes.

Desilu Productions went on to produce hit shows including *Star Trek* and *Mission: Impossible*. Although Lucy and Desi divorced in 1960, the two remained friends until Desi's death in 1986. Lucy passed away in 1989, but the laughter she shared with the world still resonates today.

(Far bottom) An I Love Lucy *mural painted by Jerry Ragg*

(Below) Lucille Ball and Desi Arnaz sit in directors' chairs at a press conference, 1953.

(Above) A 1914 photograph of Mary Cassatt

Mary Cassatt

Mary Stevenson Cassatt was born on May 22, 1844, in Allegheny City, Pennsylvania (which today is part of Pittsburgh). Cassatt was fortunate to be born into a relatively well-to-do family that valued education, travel, and talent, and as a child she was able to extensively explore Europe, where she learned French and German and developed a love of art.

After returning to America as a teenager, Cassatt enrolled in the Pennsylvania Academy of Fine Arts, but was frustrated with the sexist instruction and attitudes she encountered at the school. So she returned to Europe, settling in Paris to study with artists Jean-Leon Gerome and Charles Chaplin. Cassatt frequently sketched and painted the lives of the farmers and peasants she encountered in the French countryside, and in 1868, her painting was accepted at the Paris Salon, an annual exhibition of art from around the world.

After a brief return to America during the Franco-Prussian War, Cassatt once again traveled to Europe to continue honing her craft. While her paintings were now regularly featured in the Salon, Cassatt became disillusioned with the way female artists were treated in the art world, often being overlooked in favor of male artists of lesser talent. She made no secret of her feelings, vociferously criticizing the Salon; as a result, her art was no longer chosen to be featured.

But in 1877, fellow artist Edgar Degas invited Cassatt to join his independent group of artists known as the Impressionists. The Impressionists organized their own art exhibition apart from the Salon, inviting a more diverse range of painters and sculptors. Cassatt was the only American in the group, and the second woman—after Berthe Morisot—to be included.

With Degas as her mentor, Cassatt's art flourished. Her preferred subjects included her family, theater, and the opera, often created in pastels with an expert proficiency. As her repertoire grew, she was especially drawn to themes of mother and child, and these became some of her most well known works.

Cassatt's eyesight began to fail in the early 1900s, forcing her to diminish her time spent at the canvas. But she was no less opinionated about women's rights, campaigning for women's suffrage and speaking out on equal treatment for her fellow female artists for the rest of her life.

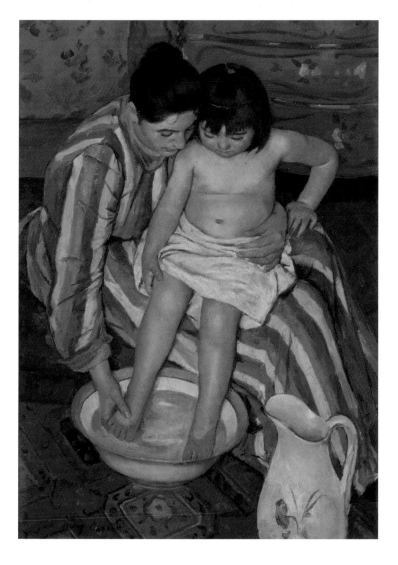

(Left) **The Child's Bath,** *1893;* *(Top left)* **The Mandolin Player,** *1872;* *(Top right)* **Margot Standing in a Garden,** *1900;* *(Bottom)* **The Boating Party,** *1893-94*

Nina Simone

Born Eunice Kathleen Waymon on February 21, 1933, in Tyron, North Carolina, Nina Simone was a natural talent who began playing the piano at only three years old. She studied classical music, giving her first recital at the age of 12 and later spending a summer studying at the Juilliard School. She then set her sights on attending the Curtis Institute of Music in Philadelphia, hoping to one day be the first famous African-American concert pianist. However, her application to the school was denied, and Simone suspected that racial prejudice was to blame.

Discouraged, Simone decided to turn away from the classical music she'd grown up on and embrace jazz and blues instead. This decision would prove to be life-changing. Simone began to sing and play piano in Atlantic City nightclubs, quickly gaining fans along the way. She recorded her first album in 1957, which included her hit "I Loves You Porgy" from the Gershwin musical *Porgy and Bess*.

Throughout the '60s and '70s, Simone released dozens of albums, often covering popular songs and putting her own soulful spin on them. She also became a prominent civil rights activist during this time, penning songs like "Mississippi Goddam" and "Young, Gifted, and Black" in response to the racial upheaval in the country.

(Left) This eight-foot bronze statue of Simone is located in her birthplace, Tyron, North Carolina.

Carol Burnett

Carol Creighton Burnett was born on April 26, 1933, in San Antonio, Texas, to parents who struggled with alcoholism. A young Burnett was sent to live with her grandmother, Mabel Eudora White, who would prove to be a positive influence on the future actress.

After high school, Burnett attended UCLA, with the intention of majoring in journalism. But halfway through her first year, she decided to switch her major to theater. The shy, insecure student was a natural on stage, coaxing laughter from the audience with her cut-up antics. Burnett was hooked, and her dreams turned to musical comedy. In 1954, she left college and moved to New York to pursue her career.

Burnett's big break came from a Tony-nominated stint on Broadway starring in the musical comedy *Once Upon a Mattress*. An Emmy-winning run on the CBS variety program *The Garry Moore Show* followed, cementing Burnett's place in the comedy world.

Smartly, Burnett had a stipulation in her contract with CBS which allowed her first dibs on a comedy variety show after *The Garry Moore Show* ended, and in 1967 *The Carol Burnett Show* debuted. The program—the first of its kind hosted by a woman—was a huge hit throughout its eleven-season run, and featured an ensemble cast including Tim Conway, Harvey Korman, and Vicki Lawrence.

Burnett would end each show by tugging on her left ear, which was her way of telling her grandmother that she was doing well and she loved her. This tradition continued even after White passed away, as a tribute to the grandmother who raised her.

Rita Moreno

Rita Moreno, the talented actress, singer, and dancer, was born Rosa Dolores Alverio Marcano on December 11, 1931, in Humacao, Puerto Rico. She and her mother moved to New York City in 1936, where Moreno began taking dancing lessons. By the time she was only 13 years old, she made her Broadway debut as "Angelina"

(Above) George Chakiris, Rita Moreno, and Russ Tamblyn at the Cast Hand and Footprint Ceremony for West Side Story

in the play *Skydrift*. Although the show received dismal reviews and closed after only a week, Moreno's performance caught the eye of Hollywood scouts and soon she was steadily working in films.

Moreno's best-known performance was in the 1961 musical *West Side Story,* for which she became the first Hispanic actress to win an Oscar for Best Supporting Actress. In 1971, she joined the cast of the children's program *The Electric Company*, earning a Grammy award for the soundtrack in 1972.

In 1975, Moreno won a Tony Award for her part in the play *The Ritz*, and guest appearances on *The Muppet Show* and *The Rockford Files* earned her Emmys. Her impressive awards collection makes her one of only 15 artists to have won all four major entertainment awards.

Now in her mid-80s, Moreno continues to act, recently appearing on the Netflix comedy *One Day at a Time* and voicing the role of Abuelita on the children's show *Nina's World*.

Kathryn Bigelow

When we think of Oscar-winning directors, many greats come to mind: Steven Spielberg, Francis Ford Coppola, Clint Eastwood. But the vast majority of those names—all but one, in fact—are men. Kathryn Bigelow, who won the Oscar for Best Director for 2008's *The Hurt Locker*, is the first—and so far, only—woman to win for the category.

Bigelow was born in San Carlos, California, on November 27, 1951. A talented painter, she earned a bachelor of fine arts degree from the San Francisco Art Institute in 1972, and then set her sights on film, attending Columbia University and graduating with a master's degree in theory and criticism.

In 1981, she directed her first feature film, *The Loveless*, and followed that with the films *Near Dark* and *Blue Steel*. But it was 1991's *Point Break*, which starred Keanu Reeves and Patrick Swayze, that proved to be Bigelow's break into mainstream filmmaking. Still, the director prefers to forgo typical genre movies and embraces her own style, often infusing issues of race and politics into her films.

Sometimes criticized for being a woman who makes "violent" films, Bigelow refuses to conform to gender stereotypes. Along with her award-winning film *The Hurt Locker*, some of Bigelow's action movies include *K-19: The Widowmaker*, and *Zero Dark Thirty*.

(Top left) Bigelow speaks at the Santa Barbara International Film Festival.

(Bottom left) Mark Boal, Kathryn Bigelow, and Greg Shapiro at the 82nd Annual Academy Awards

Lady Gaga

If the name Stefani Joanne Angelina Germanotta doesn't ring a bell, perhaps her nickname, Lady Gaga, does. Gaga was born on March 28, 1986, in New York City, where she began playing the piano and singing at the age of four. Although she was accepted to the Juilliard School at the young age of 11, she instead chose to attend private Catholic school, eventually earning early admission to New York University's Tisch School of the Arts.

The talented performer eventually withdrew from school to work on creative projects, adopting the name "Lady Gaga" in homage to the Queen song "Radio

(Right) Lady Gaga arrives at the 2010 MTV Video Music Awards wearing a dress made of raw beef.

(Above) Lady Gaga and dancers performing at a concert in Milan, 2010

Ga Ga." Between 2007 and 2008, Gaga wrote and recorded her debut album, *The Fame*, with the singles "Just Dance" and "Poker Face" reaching number one in the U.S., Australia, Canada, and the U.K. Practically overnight, Gaga's unusual name was known around the world.

Since then, Gaga has released hit after hit, and has become known as much for her eccentric and provocative attire and persona as for her talent. She has also become an outspoken advocate for LGBT rights around the world, youth empowerment, and anti-bullying campaigns, and often donates proceeds from her own concerts to charities or natural disaster relief funds.

Jane Fonda

The image of Jane Fonda performing aerobics in a leotard and legwarmers is practically synonymous with the 1980s; but the actress is more than just a workout guru. Fonda, born on December 21, 1937, in New York City, first began acting in the 1950s, doing stage work and eventually breaking into film. Throughout the '60s, '70s, and '80s, the actress worked steadily in movies, winning two Oscars—one for 1971's *Klute* and another for 1978's *Coming Home*—and earning five more nominations.

While filming *The China Syndrome* in 1979, Fonda fractured her foot and was unable to take the ballet classes she'd long used to stay in shape. Instead, she began using an aerobics workout, and her love of the exercise turned into a newfound career. Over the next 15 years, Fonda released 23 workout videos, as well as five exercise books and 13 audio books.

Fonda has also been known for her sometimes-controversial political activism, supporting feminist and civil rights movements, including the Black Panthers, in the '60s and '70s, and vociferously opposing the Vietnam War.

After some time out of the spotlight in the '90s and early 2000s, Fonda returned to acting, starring in critically acclaimed shows like *The Newsroom* and *Grace and Frankie*. Even as an octogenarian, the always-active Fonda shows no signs of slowing down.

(Left) Jane Fonda is honored at the American Film Institute's Life Achievement Awards.

Ruby Bridges

Most six-year-olds go to school with few worries, beyond learning to read and write. But little Ruby Bridges had much more serious issues to tackle. Born on September 8, 1954, in Tylertown, Mississippi, Bridges and her family moved to New Orleans in 1958. Although the landmark case of *Brown v. Board of Education*—which declared that segregation in schools was unconstitutional—was decided the same year she was born, schools in the south had been slow to integrate, with many white people objecting to the idea.

The school board of New Orleans' William Frantz Elementary decided to require an entrance exam for prospective black students, hoping the school would stay all-white. But Bridges passed the exam, and on November 14, 1960, she walked into the school, accompanied by her mother and four federal marshals. Immediately, white parents pulled their children out of the school, and all but one teacher refused to teach Bridges. For an entire year, Barbara Henry, a teacher from Boston who supported integration, taught Bridges in an empty classroom.

In 1999, Bridges founded the Ruby Bridges Foundation to uphold "values of tolerance, respect, and appreciation of all differences." For her courage as a child, Bridges was awarded the Presidential Citizens Medal in 2001 by President Bill Clinton.

(Top right) Young Ruby Bridges is escorted to and from school by U.S. Marshals.

(Bottom right) Bridges gives a commencement speech in 2015.

Daisy Bates

Civil rights activist Daisy Bates—born Daisy Lee Gaston on November 11, 1914, in Huttig, Arkansas—had a childhood marked by tragedy. When Bates was still a baby, her mother was murdered by three white men. The men were never found, and Bates developed an anger and hatred for the racial injustices faced by African-Americans.

In the early 1940s, Bates married Lucius Christopher Bates, and the pair began publishing a weekly newspaper called the *Arkansas State Press*. The paper focused on issues facing blacks in Arkansas, and was one of the earliest voices in the fight for civil rights. In 1952, Bates became the president of the Arkansas chapter of the NAACP, where she used her platform to speak out against segregation.

In 1957, Bates helped the "Little Rock Nine"—a group of African-American students trying to attend the previously all-white Central High School in Little Rock after segregation was declared unconstitutional—achieve their goal. She protected and advocated for the students until President Dwight D. Eisenhower ordered federal troops to the school to uphold the law. Bates—along with the Little Rock Nine—was posthumously awarded the Congressional Gold Medal by President Bill Clinton in 1999.

Coretta Scott King

(Above) Coretta Scott King and George W. Bush meet in the Oval Office in January of 2002.

(Above) Coretta Scott King at the Democratic National Convention in 1976

The accomplishments of Coretta Scott King may often be overshadowed by those of her famous husband, Martin Luther King Jr., but King deserves recognition in her own right. Born on April 27, 1927, in Marion, Alabama, King was a talented and smart child, graduating as valedictorian of her high school class. She then earned a bachelor's degree in music and education from Antioch College in Yellow Springs, Ohio, in 1951.

King was awarded a fellowship to the New England Conservatory of Music in Boston. While there, she met her future husband, who was a doctoral candidate at Boston University School of Theology.

The pair married on June 18, 1953. Not one to remain silent in the background, King worked side-by-side with her activist husband, even though it meant giving up her own dream of becoming a classical singer.

King spent the '50s and '60s working to end inequality, taking part in the Montgomery Bus Boycott of 1955 and working to pass the 1964 Civil Rights Act. After her husband was assassinated, King founded the Martin Luther King Jr. Center for Nonviolent Social Change, which today spans 35 acres and includes a museum, Dr. King's boyhood home, and the International Civil Rights Walk of Fame.

Dorothy Height

Dorothy Irene Height was born on March 24, 1912, in Richmond, Virginia. After high school, she attended New York University, where she earned both a bachelor's degree in education and a master's degree in psychology.

Height began her career as a social worker, working at the Harlem YWCA in 1937. While there, she met Mary McLeod Bethune when she came to tour the facility, and the two struck up a friendship. This led to Height's interest in civil rights activism, and soon she joined the National Council of Negro Women.

In 1957, Height was named president of the organization, a position she would hold for an impressive 40 years. She worked with civil rights leaders like Martin Luther King Jr. and James Farmer, and stood near King when he delivered his "I Have a Dream" speech.

Despite civil rights progress, Height was dismayed by how women of all colors were dismissed and demeaned by their male counterparts, and soon began fighting for women's rights, as well. In 1971, she was a founding member of the National Women's Political Caucus, along with Gloria Steinem, Betty Friedan, and Shirley Chisholm.

For her activism work, Height was awarded the Presidential Medal of Freedom in 1994 and the Congressional Gold Medal in 2004.

(Bottom right) Dorothy Height and Eleanor Roosevelt in 1960

Mary McLeod Bethune

The daughter of former slaves, Mary Jane McLeod Bethune was born on July 10, 1875, in a tiny log cabin in Mayesville, South Carolina, the fifteenth of seventeen children. Many of her siblings had been born into slavery before the 13th Amendment abolished the practice in 1865. The entire family worked on their rice and cotton farm to earn enough to maintain their independence; but Bethune desired an education, just like the white children she knew.

Bethune began attending school—the only child in her family to do so—when a missionary opened a school for African-American children five miles away from her family's farm. She walked each day to and from the schoolhouse, and would then share what she'd learned with her family. Later, Bethune received a scholarship to attend Scotia Seminary (now Barber-Scotia College) and then studied at Dwight Moody's Institute for Home and Foreign Missions (now Moody Bible Institute).

Bethune began a career as a teacher, wanting to share her love of education with other black Americans. In 1899, she moved to Palatka, Florida, to run a mission school, and in 1904, with a decade of teaching experience under her belt, she founded the Daytona Normal and Industrial Institute for Negro Girls in Daytona. Starting with only five girls, Bethune scraped by with meager resources and donations from local businesses until her school grew, little by little, to more than 250 students.

When lobbying for donations for her school Bethune became acquainted with business owners, benefactors, and politicians. She started lending her expertise to government causes, advising presidents Calvin Coolidge and Herbert Hoover, and in 1935 became a special advisor to President Franklin D. Roosevelt on minority affairs.

Bethune passed away in 1955, after spending the majority of her life devoted to social causes, and in 1973, she was inducted into the National Women's Hall of Fame. Befitting of someone with such passion for education, dozens of schools around the country have been named in her honor.

(Opposite page, top) A photo of Mary McLeod Bethune and students from the Daytona Normal and Industrial Institute for Negro Girls, taken circa 1905

(Right) Mary McLeod Bethune Council Home in Washington, D.C. The home is on the National Register of Historic Places. It is open to the public as a museum focusing on Bethune's legacy.

Claudette Colvin

Most Americans believe that Rosa Parks was the first person to be arrested for refusing to give up her bus seat to a white passenger; but that distinction actually belongs to fellow civil rights activist Claudette Colvin.

Colvin was born in Montgomery, Alabama, on September 5, 1939. As a teenager, she took the bus every day to attend the segregated Booker T. Washington High School, where she was known as an excellent student who hoped to be president one day. On March 2, 1955—nine months before Rosa Parks' famous act—the driver of Colvin's bus demanded she give up her seat to a white woman. The 15-year-old refused, saying it was her constitutional right to sit where she chose.

For her refusal, Colvin was arrested and charged with violating the city's segregation laws. The NAACP considered using the teenager's case as an example of why such laws should be abolished, but decided not to draw attention to her due to her young age.

Colvin went on to be one of the plaintiffs in the case of *Browder v. Gayle*, which, in 1956, ruled that Montgomery's bus segregation was unconstitutional.

(Left) A photo of Claudette Colvin at age 13, taken in 1953

Fannie Lou Hamer

Fannie Lou Hamer—born Fannie Lou Townsend on October 6, 1917, in Montgomery County, Mississippi—was the youngest of 20 children born to sharecroppers. She was a good student and an avid reader, but dropped out of school at the age of 12 to work full time and help care for her aging parents. She married Perry "Pap" Hamer in 1944, and the two worked together on a cotton plantation.

In 1962, Hamer attended a meeting held by the Student Nonviolent Coordinating Committee, where she and other African-Americans were encouraged to register to vote. Although it was their right, blacks in the south were frequently met with violent opposition when attempting to register to vote. When Hamer's boss found out that she'd tried to register herself, she was immediately fired from the job she'd held for two decades.

Instead of being discouraged, Hamer decided to dedicate the rest of her life to the fight for civil rights. She focused on voter registration, increasing business opportunities for minorities, and advocated for property ownership. She also co-founded the National Women's Political Caucus in 1971, believing women of all races could be a powerful voice in politics. Hamer was inducted into the National Women's Hall of Fame in 1993.

Rosa Parks

Rosa Louise McCauley was born on February 4, 1913, in Tuskegee, Alabama. As a child, she regularly saw the racism that became a way of life in the south, where public facilities, stores, schools, and transportation were all segregated according to skin color. In 1932, she married Raymond Parks, a member of the NAACP who was active in the civil rights movement.

Over the next decade, Parks became more active in the movement herself, joining the Montgomery chapter of the NAACP in 1943. She served as youth leader and secretary to President E.D. Nixon until 1957. But her defining moment occurred on December 1, 1955, after she'd put in a long day's work as a seamstress at a department store. On her bus ride home, Parks was asked to move so a white passenger could take her seat, but she refused. She would later say that her refusal was not because she was physically tired, but rather, "tired of giving in."

Parks was arrested and charged with violating the city's segregation laws, and was later bailed out of jail by NAACP leader Nixon and lawyer Clifford Durr. That same evening, Nixon began plans for a bus boycott in Montgomery, which he organized to begin on December 5—the day of Parks' trial.

Parks was found guilty and fined $10; but on the same day, 35,000 leaflets were distributed advertising the bus boycott. With more than 75 percent of Montgomery's bus passengers being African-American, the buses in the city were nearly empty for all of the boycott's 381 days. The city's transit company lost a huge amount

of revenue, with many buses simply sitting idle.

On November 13, 1956, the Supreme Court ruled that racial segregation laws were unconstitutional, and the boycott officially ended on December 20 that year. Parks may not have been the first to refuse to give up her seat, but her actions were the catalyst.

(Top left) The bus where Rosa Parks made her historic stand against segregation is now located at the Henry Ford Museum in Detroit.

(Bottom left) A sculpture of Rosa Parks at the National Civil Rights Museum

(Bottom right) President Bill Clinton presents Parks with the Presidential Medal of Freedom in 1996.

Sojourner Truth

Born into slavery in 1797 in Swartekill, New York, Sojourner Truth was sold to four different masters in her younger years. Although New York sought to outlaw slavery in 1799, the state was slow to follow through, not officially emancipating slaves until 1827. A year earlier, Truth escaped with her infant daughter, Sophia, taking refuge with an abolitionist couple.

After the New York State Emancipation Act took effect, Truth went to work as a housekeeper, first for Christian evangelist Elijah Pierson and then for religious leader Robert Matthews. She became a devout Methodist, and in 1843 she changed her name from her birth name—Isabella Baumfree—to Sojourner Truth, to reflect her desire to travel and preach on the abolition of slavery.

In 1851, at the Ohio Women's Rights Convention, Truth delivered her famous "Ain't I a Woman?" speech, calling for equal rights for women and blacks. Using her clout as a well-known abolitionist, Truth was able to recruit many black soldiers for the Union Army during the Civil War. Even after the war was over, she continued fighting for equality, advocating for property rights for former slaves.

Truth impressed many reformers during her time, including Wendell Phillips and Susan B. Anthony, who remained her friends for the rest of her life.

(Right) A portrait of Sojourner Truth.

Elizabeth Cady Stanton

The daughter of a prominent lawyer, Elizabeth Cady Stanton—born November 12, 1815, in Johnstown, New York—read her father's law books even as a child. She was struck by the disparity between men and women in legal matters, and was dismayed that married women were allowed no property or income. After graduating from the Troy Female Seminary in 1832, it was only natural that Stanton was drawn to activism.

She met her husband, Henry Brewster Stanton, through her work with abolitionist movements; true to her belief in women's equality, she omitted "obey" from their marriage vows. The couple had seven children and settled in Seneca Falls, New York. It was here that Stanton helped to organize the Seneca Falls Convention, a gathering of more than 300 people where she read her "Declaration of Sentiments," which proclaimed the equality of the sexes.

In the early 1850s, Stanton met Susan B. Anthony and the two struck up a lifelong friendship, often working together to promote women's suffrage. A great orator, Stanton wrote many of Anthony's speeches. She wasn't afraid to speak out on "taboo" subjects of the day, including divorce, birth control, and interracial marriage. Today, Stanton's house in Seneca Falls is a National Historic Landmark—and a reminder of her fight for equality.

Harriet Tubman

(Above) Harriet Tubman, far left, stands with her family and neighbors in Auburn, New York, circa 1885.

Perhaps the most famous abolitionist of all time, Harriet Tubman—born Araminta Ross sometime around 1822—was the daughter of slaves from Dorchester County, Maryland. Tubman endured much hardship in her early life, being severely mistreated by several masters. She was often beaten and whipped, but her worst injury occurred when an angry overseer threw a two-pound weight at her, striking her in the head. As a result, Tubman suffered seizures, headaches, and narcolepsy for the rest of her life.

In 1849, Tubman's owner died, and she saw it as an opportunity to escape. Using the Underground Railroad—a network of safe houses and secret routes created by abolitionists and other activists to help slaves reach free states—Tubman traveled nearly 90 miles to Philadelphia. But instead of remaining in the safety of the free state of Pennsylvania, Tubman made it her mission to rescue other slaves, starting with her niece, Kessiah, in Baltimore. Tubman was able to guide Kessiah and her family back to Philadelphia, then she returned to Maryland to retrieve her parents and siblings.

Quickly earning the nickname "Moses" for her leadership and guidance, Tubman continued to help escaped slaves even after the passage of the Fugitive Slave Law in 1850. The law stated that escaped slaves found in free states could be returned to slavery, forcing even anti-slavery law enforcement officials to aid in the capture of escaped slaves. To combat this new obstacle, Tubman rerouted the Underground Railroad into Canada.

During the Civil War, Tubman worked as a cook and nurse for the Union Army. But she was never one to stay on the sidelines, and her knowledge of covert travel was soon put to use when she became the first woman to lead an armed assault in the war. Tubman guided the Combahee River Raid in South Carolina, helping to free more than 700 slaves.

After her death in 1913, Tubman was buried with military honors at Fort Hill Cemetery in Auburn, New York. She is considered an American icon, with dozens of schools, many monuments—and even an asteroid—named in her honor.

(Bottom left) Tubman's residence in Auburn, New York, is now part of the Harriet Tubman National Historical Park, a park consisting of three properties associated with the life of Harriet Tubman.

MRS. WOODHULL ASSERTING HER RIGHT TO VOTE.—[FROM A SKETCH BY H. BALLING.]

Because of her experience with her ex-husband, Woodhull became dismayed that women were often trapped in loveless marriages or ostracized if they chose divorce. She began advocating for women's rights, and spoke out about women's suffrage, social reform, and even birth control.

In 1872, Woodhull ran for president under the newly formed Equal Rights Party, causing even more of a stir when she nominated abolitionist Frederick Douglass to be her vice president. The interracial pair were not a popular ticket; but Woodhull, clearly a woman ahead of her time, was not afraid to fight for what she believed in.

Victoria Woodhull

Hillary Clinton may have made history in 2016 by becoming the first woman to run for president on a major party ticket, but women's rights activist Victoria Woodhull was the very first female presidential hopeful—nearly a century and a half earlier.

Woodhull was born on September 23, 1838, in Homer, Ohio. She had a difficult childhood, with an illiterate mother and a con man father who burned his own gristmill in an attempt to collect insurance money. Woodhull married 28-year-old Canning Woodhull when she was only 15, soon discovering her husband was an alcoholic womanizer. They divorced ten years later, even though divorce was considered a scandalous option at the time.

Abigail Adams

Born on November 22, 1744—32 years before the creation of the United States—Abigail Smith grew up in Weymouth, Massachusetts, still considered a British colony at the time. She married John Adams on October 25, 1764, although her mother disapproved of the match, thinking the future-president was not cultured enough for her daughter.

John Adams became active in forming the new government of the country, and Abigail was often vocal to her husband about her own political beliefs, reminding him not to overlook women's issues. When he became the first vice president in 1789, Abigail divided her time between the capital and their farm, where she made sure the operation ran smoothly and took care of business matters.

In 1797, John Adams became president; Abigail was such a confidante and support for her husband that she was called "Mrs. President" by critics, who often felt women had no place in politics. But their correspondence during this time shows that John often asked for her advice on everything from foreign relations to immigration. Abigail was also a staunch advocate for women's rights and ending slavery.

In the first years of the fledging United States, Abigail Adams was already paving the way for future women in politics.

(Right) An oil painting of Abigail Adams at age 56

Hariet Beecher Stowe

Harriet Elizabeth Beecher was born on June 14, 1811, in Litchfield, Connecticut. Her father, a preacher who strongly opposed slavery, and his abolitionist views influenced all of his 13 children, and in 1832 Hariet met like-minded seminary teacher Calvin Ellis Stowe when she joined a literary association. The two married in 1836, and moved to Brunswick, Maine.

Stowe and her husband were supporters of the Underground Railroad, housing several fugitive slaves before their escape into Canada. Already sympathetic to their cause, Stowe's feelings grew more pronounced after the loss of her eighteen-month-old son, Samuel. Having a new understanding of pain and loss prompted her to pen a story about the injustices of slavery.

In June of 1851, the first installment of *Uncle Tom's Cabin* was published in the anti-slavery journal *The National Era*. Stowe's emotional story of the devastating impact of slavery on families and children was published in installments until April 1852. On March 20, 1852, the story was published in book form, with an initial print run of 5,000 copies. But the story was so popular that in less than a year, it had sold 300,000 copies.

Stowe's goal was to educate northerners—who were often ignorant of the evils of slavery—of what was occurring in the south. Her book touched off a debate between the pro-slavery South and the abolitionist North, and after the Civil War began she traveled to Washington, D.C., to meet with President Abraham Lincoln. According to legend, the president greeted her by saying, "So you are the little woman who wrote the book that started this great war."

Three years after its publication, *Uncle Tom's Cabin* was called "the most popular novel of our day"—only the Bible sold more copies. Stowe's house in Brunswick, Maine, where she wrote the influential work, has been restored and is now a museum open to the public.

UNCLE TOM'S CABIN;

OR,

LIFE AMONG THE LOWLY.

BY

HARRIET BEECHER STOWE.

VOL. I.

ONE HUNDRED AND FIFTH THOUSAND.

BOSTON:
JOHN P. JEWETT & COMPANY
CLEVELAND, OHIO:
JEWETT, PROCTOR & WORTHINGTON.
1852.

(Above) A first edition of Uncle Tom's Cabin

Susan B. Anthony

Susan Anthony was born into a family of Quakers on February 15, 1820, in Adams, Massachusetts. Interestingly, she chose the "B" initial in her name herself, as an homage to her aunt, Susan Brownell. Anthony's father believed that all of his children—girls as well as boys—should learn responsibilities and be self-sufficient. So when her family began to struggle financially after the Panic of 1837, Anthony took it upon herself to find work, teaching at a Quaker boarding school.

In the mid-1840s, the Anthony family moved to a farm near Rochester, New York, where they became active in the abolitionist movement. The farm became a meeting place for those devoted to the cause, including famed abolitionist Frederick Douglass. Anthony moved away from the farm for several years to be the headmistress of the Canajoharie Academy in Canajoharie, New York. While there, she began moving away from the Quaker beliefs she had always been taught and started embracing ideas of social reform.

After the Canajoharie Academy closed, Anthony started getting more involved in reform issues. In 1851, she met Elizabeth Cady Stanton at an anti-slavery conference. The pair eventually formed the New York State Woman's Rights Committee, lobbying for women to have the right to own property and vote.

Anthony also joined the American Anti-Slavery Society, fighting for an end to slavery until the Civil War broke out.

After the war, Anthony focused more on women's rights, forming the American Equal Rights Association in 1866. She and Stanton also founded the National Woman Suffrage Association in 1869. Anthony even illegally voted in the 1872 presidential election, for which she was fined $100, but never paid.

Sadly, Anthony died 14 years before the 19th Amendment—which gave women the right to vote—was passed in 1920. For her many efforts, she was honored with the Susan B. Anthony dollar coin in 1979—making her the first woman to be featured on a U.S. coin.

(Below left) A portrait of Susan B. Anthony taken between 1880 and 1906

(Below right) A portrait of Anthony from the 1890s

Shirley Ann Jackson

(Above) Shirley Ann Jackson speaks at the Annual Meeting of the New Champions in Tianjin, China, in 2010. The same year, Jackson accepted a ten-year contract renewal as president of Rensselear Polytechnic Institute. The decision was made unanimously by the Rensselaer Board of Trustees.

Shirley Ann Jackson was born on August 5, 1946, in Washington, D.C. A lover of science at an early age, she graduated as high school valedictorian and then attended the Massachusetts Institute of Technology, where she studied theoretical physics and elementary particle theory. In 1973, she received a PhD in nuclear physics, becoming the first African-American woman to earn a doctorate at MIT.

Jackson completed years of postdoctoral research at laboratories including Fermilab in Batavia, Illinois, and CERN, the European Organization for Nuclear Research, in Switzerland. She then worked at AT&T Bell Laboratories for 15 years. After serving on the faculty of Rutgers University for four years, Jackson was appointed to the U.S. Nuclear Regulatory Commission by President Bill Clinton. In 1999, she became president of Rensselaer Polytechnic Institute (RPI) in Troy, New York, where she has helped to raise more than $1 billion for charitable causes.

In addition to her doctorate from MIT, Jackson has achieved several "firsts" as an African-American woman: She was the first to be elected president and then chairman of the American Association for the Advancement of Science, the first to be president of RPI, and in 2014, became the first to win the National Medal of Science.

Nancy J. Currie-Gregg

Born Nancy J. Decker on December 29, 1958, in Wilmington, Delaware, Nancy J. Currie-Gregg has the distinction of being in an exclusive club of female astronauts. Of the more than 500 people who have traveled to space, only 61 have been women—45 of those women have been American.

Currie-Gregg's impressive resume begins with a bachelor's degree in biological science from Ohio State University, a master's degree in safety engineering from the University of Southern California, and a doctorate in industrial engineering from the University of Houston. If that isn't inspiring enough, she is also a retired United States Army colonel and Master Army Aviator who has flown more than 4,000 hours in rotary-wing and fixed-wing aircraft.

Currie-Gregg was chosen to be an astronaut in 1990, and completed four space shuttle missions—*Endeavour, Discovery,* and *Columbia*—amounting to more than 1,000 hours in space, where she conducted biomedical experiments, traveled to the International Space Station, and helped to service the Hubble Space Telescope.

Now a principle engineer in the NASA Engineering and Safety Center, Currie-Gregg has accumulated a long list of awards, including the Legion of Merit and the NASA Outstanding Leadership Medal.

Grace Hopper

With the nickname "Amazing Grace," it's no surprise that Grace Hopper's life was full of notable achievements. Born in New York City on December 9, 1906, Hopper had an early interest in mathematics and physics, which she studied at Vassar College. She went on to earn a PhD in mathematics from Yale University in 1934, at a time when few women pursued such a subject.

Hopper began her career as a college professor, teaching mathematics at Vassar. But when World War II broke out, she decided to join the Navy Reserve, where her mathematics expertise led to an assignment programing Mark I computers. After the war, Hopper continued studying computer programing with the Navy Reserve, and then moved into private industry, working with companies that oversaw the development of the UNIVAC computer—the first commercial computer available in the United States. Hopper and her team also created the first compiler—a software program that translates programming languages.

Hopper's genius with computers made her an indispensable member of the Navy, where she worked for 42 years. She finished her military career with the rank of rear admiral—becoming not only one of the Navy's few female admirals, but also retiring as the oldest active-duty commissioned officer in the Navy, at 79 years old.

(Below right) Grace Hopper sits at the UNIVAC keyboard, circa 1960.

Katherine Johnson

(Above left) Katherine Johnson at NASA Langley Research Center in 1985

(Above right) Katherine Johnson in 1966

Born on August 26, 1918, in White Sulphur Springs, West Virginia, Katherine Coleman Johnson was an exceptionally bright child who started high school at the age of 10. She then enrolled in West Virginia State College, and at 18—the age when most students are just beginning college—Johnson graduated summa cum laude with degrees in mathematics and French.

Johnson did some graduate work at West Virginia University, becoming one of only three African-American students chosen to desegregate the graduate school. Although she did not complete the program, Johnson continued on a path toward a career as a research mathematician. In 1952, after a decade of teaching, she was selected to work for the National Advisory Committee for Aeronautics (NACA), and later for the Langley Research Center in Hampton, Virginia.

In the late '50s, NACA became NASA, and Johnson tackled her most notable work: plotting the path of space flights. Her accurate, precise calculations proved crucial for helping to safely launch and return spacecraft, including Alan Shepard's first flight to space, John Glenn's orbit around Earth, the Apollo 11 mission to the moon, and the fateful Apollo 13 mission.

In 2015, Johnson was awarded the Presidential Medal of Freedom. Her story was turned into the 2016 Oscar-nominated film, *Hidden Figures*.

Lisa Randall

Born on June 18, 1962, in New York City, Lisa Randall's love of science began at an early age. She enjoyed the objective nature of math classes over the subjective nature of English classes, preferring problems with clear-cut answers. But math didn't satisfy her curiosity about the physical world; after taking her first physics class in high school, she knew she'd found her true calling.

At the age of 18, Randall won first place in the Westinghouse Science Talent Search—a competition once described by President George H.W. Bush as "the Super Bowl of science" —and embarked on a scientific career path. She attended Harvard University, where she eventually earned a PhD in theoretical particle physics.

Now a professor at Harvard—where she was the first tenured female theoretical physicist—Randall has written two popular books, *Warped Passages* and *Knocking on Heaven's Door*, to share her love of science with a general audience in an accessible way. Her hope is that that people will no longer think of the science world as a man-only field, but rather one where women are also leaders in research and new discoveries.

(Right) Lisa Randall at a conference in Genoa, Italy, 2006

Susan Solomon

Climate change has been a hot topic (no pun intended) in recent decades, and we may have atmospheric chemist Susan Solomon to thank for bringing it to the forefront of discussion. Solomon, born in Chicago, Illinois, in 1956, got hooked on science as a child, watching shows like *The Undersea World of Jacques Cousteau*. She studied chemistry at the Illinois Institute of Technology, and then earned a PhD in chemistry from the University of California, Berkeley.

In 1981, Solomon joined the National Oceanic and Atmospheric Administration (NOAA), where she began researching whether there was a connection between compounds called chlorofluorocarbons (CFCs) and a hole in the Antarctic ozone layer. As the leader of a team of scientists—and the only woman—who traveled to Antarctica in 1986, Solomon was able to prove the relation between CFCs and ozone depletion. Her work led to the 1987 Montreal Protocol, which called for United Nations countries to reduce use of ozone-depleting chemicals.

Solomon spent 30 years working for NOAA, then joined the faculty at MIT as a professor of atmospheric chemistry and climate science. In 2007, she—along with the Intergovernmental Panel on Climate Change and former vice president Al Gore—won a Nobel Peace Prize for her research.

(Bottom left) Susan Soloman (third from right) and other recipients of the 2007 Nobel Award meet with President George W. Bush in the Oval Office, 2007.

Sally Ride

(Above) Sally Ride was one of five astronaut crewmembers on the Challenger's second orbital mission in 1983.

Sally Kristen Ride was born on May 26, 1951, in Los Angeles, California, where she attended the Westlake School for Girls on a scholarship and was a nationally ranked tennis player. But science was her first love, and she earned bachelor's degrees in both English and physics from Stanford University, then a master's degree and a PhD in physics.

In 1978, the same year she received her PhD, Ride applied to join NASA's astronaut program, and beat out 1,000 other hopefuls for a spot. She began her NASA career as a ground-based flight controller,

but in 1983, after undergoing rigorous training, Ride got her chance to go into space. Brushing off sexist questions and comments from the media, Ride's only concern was to perform her job as best she could; and on June 18, 1983, she became the first American woman to go to space, as a member of the *Challenger* crew.

Ride travelled to space again in 1984, and was scheduled for a third trip; sadly, the *Challenger* disaster on January 28, 1986, grounded her permanently. She served on the commission that investigated the space shuttle explosion, and later served on the commission that investigated the *Columbia* disaster—the only person to serve on both panels.

After NASA, Ride became the director of the California Space Institute at the University of California, San Diego, and taught physics at the school. In 2001, she founded Sally Ride Science, a company that creates educational products to inspire young people interested in STEM (science, technology, engineering, math) careers, focusing especially on girls.

Although Ride passed away in 2012 after a battle with pancreatic cancer, her legacy continues to inspire. She has received numerous awards and honors, including the National Space Society's von Braun Award and the Lindbergh Eagle Award, and inductions into the National Women's Hall of Fame and the Astronaut Hall of Fame. While women in STEM careers make up less than 25 percent of those who pursue them, the numbers continue to grow—thanks in part to groundbreaking women like Sally Ride.

(Bottom right) Sally Ride communicates with ground controllers while on the **Challenger** *mission.*

Ellen Ochoa

Selected by NASA in 1990, Ellen Ochoa—born May 10, 1958, in Los Angeles, California—became the first Hispanic female astronaut in July 1991. On the road to NASA, she earned a bachelor's degree in physics from San Diego State University and a master's and doctorate degree in electrical engineering from Stanford University.

In 1993, Ochoa became the first Hispanic woman to go into space, as a member of a *Discovery* mission to study the Earth's ozone layer. In all, Ochoa took four space flights, where she served as a mission specialist and flight engineer. She logged almost 1,000 hours in space before retiring from space flight in 2007, then went on to serve as deputy director of the Johnson Space Center in Houston, Texas. In 2013, she broke barriers again, becoming the first Hispanic—and only the second female—director of the center.

Ochoa's many awards include NASA's Exceptional Service Medal and an Outstanding Leadership Medal. Several schools in the country have been named in her honor, and in 2017, she was inducted into the United States Astronaut Hall of Fame.

(Left) Ochoa plays the flute in the flight deck of Discovery. *In addition to being an astronaut, Ochoa is a classical floutist,and she has played with the Stanford Symphony Orchestra.*

Rachel Carson

(Above left) Rachel Carson and Bob Hines conduct marine biology research in the Atlantic Ocean, 1952.

Born on a farm near Springdale, Pennsylvania, on May 27, 1907, Rachel Carson grew up with first-hand knowledge of farming, nature, and animals. She loved reading and writing about animals, and her first story was published when she was only 10 years old.

Carson was torn between her two loves—writing and nature—when she began studying at the Pennsylvania College for Women (now Chatham College), first majoring in English, then switching to biology. In 1935, she went to work for the U.S. Bureau of Fisheries, where she wrote copy for educational radio programs that explored aquatic life. Especially passionate about the sea, Carson wrote a trilogy of books

about the ocean— 1941's *Under the Sea Wind*, 1951's *The Sea Around Us*, and 1955's *The Edge of the Sea*—that described sea life in clear and non-technical prose. *The Sea Around Us* was on the *New York Times* Best Seller list for 86 weeks and won the National Book Award for nonfiction.

But it was her 1962 book, *Silent Spring*, that proved to be the most popular. The book warned of the indiscriminate use of pesticides and, in 2012, was declared a National Historic Chemical Landmark for its influence on the modern environmental movement.

Serena Williams

Serena Jameka Williams was born on September 26, 1981, in Saginaw, Michigan. She began playing tennis at the age of three, practicing for two hours a day with her father. By the time she was nine, she was ranked first in the 10-and-under division on the United States Tennis Association tour. Williams and her family then moved to West Palm Beach, Florida, so that she and her equally-famous sister, Venus, could attend a tennis academy.

Williams turned pro in 1995, when she was only 14 years old. A year before she graduated from high school, she was already gaining popularity and competing in tournaments, and she was ranked No. 99 in the world. Advertisers took notice

of this rising star, and soon after graduating from high school, Williams nailed down an impressive $12 million deal with shoe giant Puma.

Williams and her sister often played against each other, their wins and losses going back and forth like the tennis balls they hit. But in 2002, Williams beat Venus in the finals of Wimbledon, the U.S. Open, and the French Open, and in 2003 she won the Australian Open. Holding all four titles at the same time, she dubbed her wins the "Serena Slam."

After her stellar year, Williams was faced with difficulties. She was plagued by injuries, underwent knee surgery, and dealt with the tragic murder of her half-sister, Yetunde Price. Burned out, her ranking fell to 139. But after a life-changing trip to Africa that helped her embrace "forgiveness and moving on," Williams made a comeback in 2008, winning the U.S. Open and regaining her top place in the rankings.

Williams has won a total of 23 Grand Slam singles titles, but tennis isn't the only important aspect of her life. She and Venus are active in charity work, often teaming up for philanthropic projects. But most important is her daughter, Alexis Olympia Ohanian, born in 2017 to Williams and her husband, Reddit co-founder Alexis Ohanian.

(Top left) Serena Williams at her final match of the Australian open in Melbourne, Australia, 2016

(Bottom left) Williams prepares a serve at the 2016 U.S. Open Grand Slam tournament.

Mia Hamm

It may be surprising to learn that the person often considered the best female soccer player in history was born with a clubfoot. But Mariel Margaret Hamm, born March 17, 1972, in Selma, Alabama, had to wear casts on her feet as a child to correct the issue. The daughter of an Air Force pilot, Hamm and her family often moved to different locations around the world. While living in Florence, Italy, as a toddler, Hamm was introduced to soccer, and the sport would go on to shape her entire life.

At 15, Hamm became the youngest player to play for the U.S. women's national soccer team. She then attended the University of North Carolina at Chapel Hill, where she helped lead the school's team to four consecutive NCAA women's championships.

A 19-year-old Hamm was on the 1991 team that won the FIFA Women's World Cup, once again becoming the youngest player to do so. Hamm and her teammates went on to win the gold at the 1996 Olympics, won the 1999 World Cup, and won another gold at the 2004 Olympics.

In 2013, Hamm was the first woman to be inducted into the World Football Hall of Fame in Pachuca, Mexico.

Wilma Rudolph

Born into poverty on June 23, 1940, in Saint Bethlehem, Tennessee, Wilma Rudolph was a sickly child who suffered from pneumonia, scarlet fever, and polio. The polio weakened her left leg and foot, and she spent much of her childhood wearing a brace and undergoing treatments to strengthen her leg.

Showing great determination, Rudolph learned to walk without the brace by the time she was 12. But she didn't just walk—she ran, joining the track and basketball teams in high school. When she was only 16, she qualified for the 1956 Olympics in Melbourne, Australia, where she won a bronze medal in the 4 x 100 meters relay.

Rudolph continued competing in track at Tennessee State University, training hard for the 1960 Olympics in Rome, Italy. During an unusually hot summer where the temperature climbed close to 110 degrees Fahrenheit, Rudolph managed to set records in the 100- and 200-meter dash, and the 4 x 100 meter relay, and won three gold medals. She was nicknamed "The Tornado, the fastest woman on earth."

The once polio-stricken Randolph became a source of inspiration for generations of athletes. She retired from running at the age of 22, preferring to teach, coach, and provide support to youth athletes.

Billie Jean King

Billie Jean King—born Billie Jean Moffitt on November 22, 1943, in Long Beach, California—loved sports as a child, and excelled at softball. But when her conservative parents suggested she take up a more "ladylike" sport, King settled on tennis.

Her talent for the game was evident immediately. Playing in various tournaments as a teenager, King first made headlines in 1961, when the 17-year-old paired up with 18-year-old Karen Hantze Susmen and the duo became the youngest team to win a Wimbledon doubles title. She continued to play while attending California State University, Los Angeles, but after three years decided to drop out of school and focus on tennis full time.

The late '60s and early '70s were King's best competitive years, with six Wimbledon titles, four U.S. Open titles, one French Open title, and one Australian Championship title. From 1966 through 1975, she was ranked No. 1 in the world six times, No. 2 three times, and No. 3 once.

But perhaps her most famous match was not for a Grand Slam title, but rather for bragging rights. In 1973, former men's champion Bobby Riggs declared that even at 55 years old, he could handily beat any female tennis player. King upped his challenge by suggesting they play for a $100,000 prize in an exhibition game.

In what became known as the "Battle of the Sexes," King and Riggs played in a packed Houston Astrodome, in a game broadcast to 90 million

(Left) A photograph of Billie Jean King taken in 1978

television viewers. King won, and decades later the spectacle was turned into a 2017 movie starring Emma Stone and Steve Carrell.

King used her popularity within the sport to advocate for equal pay and prize money for male and female tennis players, even threatening a boycott of the 1973 U.S. Open if they didn't address the issue. Subsequently, the U.S. Open became the first major tennis tournament to pay both sexes equally.

Before retiring in 1990, King won 39 championships, including a record-breaking 20 at Wimbledon. She has remained an advocate for the sport and for gender equality, and was awarded the Presidential Medal of Freedom in 2009.

(Bottom left) A postage stamp featuring Billie Jean King, circa 1988

(Bottom middle) Billie Jean King and Bobby Riggs during the 1973 "Battle of the Sexes"

(Bottom right) King at the opening ceremony of the 2006 U.S. Open

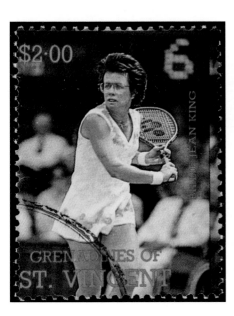

Jackie Joyner-Kersee

(Above) A postage stamp from 1989 featuring Jackie Joyner-Kersee

(Above) Joyner-Kersee poses with Secretary of Defense Ash Carter at the Pentagon Athletic Center in 2015.

The daughter of teenage parents who named her after Jacqueline Kennedy, Jacqueline Joyner-Kersee was born on March 3, 1962, in East St. Louis, Illinois. Although her family struggled financially, Joyner-Kersee excelled at sports—including track, basketball, and volleyball—enabling her to attend the University of California at Los Angeles on a full scholarship.

Joyner-Kersee participated in both track and basketball while in college, becoming one of UCLA's all-time greatest players in the sport. But in 1983, she set basketball aside so she could train for the heptathlon at the 1984 Olympics. The year was the first that the Olympics included women's heptathlon, which is made up of seven track and field events. Each event is rated on a scoring system; in the 1984 Games, Joyner-Kersee earned a silver medal, five points behind the gold medalist, Australian Glynis Nunn.

After graduating from UCLA in 1985, Joyner-Kersee returned to training for the heptathlon, competing in the 1988 Olympics and scoring a record-breaking 7,291 points in the seven events, making her the first American woman to win a gold medal in heptathlon. Just days later, she broke another record, jumping 7.4 meters in the long jump and becoming the first woman to win gold in the event.

After retiring in 2001, Joyner-Kersee created the Jackie Joyner-Kersee Youth Center Foundation in her hometown of East St. Louis to encourage youth participation in sports, and helped found Athletes for Hope—along with Andre Agassi, Muhammad Ali, and Mia Hamm—that helps professional athletes team up with charities and philanthropic causes.

In all, Joyner-Kersee won three gold, one silver, and two bronze Olympic medals, four World Championship gold medals, and a Pan American Games gold medal. She still holds the world record in heptathlon, and *Sports Illustrated* named her the greatest female athlete of the 20th century. In 2004, Joyner-Kersee was inducted into the USA Track & Field Hall of Fame.

(Far right) Joyner-Kersee at The Paley Honors: Celebrating Women in Television at Cipriani Wall Street, 2017

(Right) Joyner-Kersee at the World Junior Championships in Athletics in 2014

Althea Gibson

The daughter of sharecroppers from Silver, South Carolina, Althea Gibson was born on August 25, 1927, and grew up in New York City. Gibson loved sports and was so good at table tennis that she was encouraged to play tennis on a court.

Only a year after she picked up her first tennis racket, she won a tournament sponsored by the American Tennis Association. Between 1944 and 1956, Gibson lost just one title with the ATA, in 1946.

In the middle of this great success, Gibson was often barred from competing in segregated tournaments. But her talent was impossible to deny: In 1950, she was finally invited to compete at the U.S. National Championships—now the U.S. Open—becoming the first African-American to do so. She made history again in 1951 as the first black player at Wimbledon. By 1953, she was one of the top ten tennis players in the United States, but she had yet to win a Grand Slam title.

But that changed in 1956, when Gibson became the first African-American to win the French Open. This was followed by Wimbledon and U.S. Open titles in 1957 and 1958. In total, Gibson won 56 singles and doubles championships before turning pro in 1959.

(Top left) Althea Gibson holds a tennis racquet, 1955.

(Bottom left) Darlene Hard gives Althea Gibson a congratulatory kiss after Gibson wins the 1956 Wimbledon Women's Singles Championship. The Wimbledon trophy was presented to Gibson by Queen Elizabeth II.

Florence Griffith Joyner

Known to her fans as "Flo-Jo," Florence Delorez Griffith—who, in 1987, married Jackie Joyner-Kersee's brother, Al Joyner—was born in Los Angeles, California, on December 21, 1959. She began running at the age of 7, and it soon became apparent that she had a gift for speed. Joyner won the Jesse Owens National Youth Games at the age of 14, and again at 15, and then became a track star at the University of California at Los Angeles.

While in college, Joyner won NCAA championships in 1982, in the 200-meter event, and 1983, in the 400-meter event. She next set her sights on the Olympics, where she made her debut in 1984. Joyner immediately made an impression, wearing form-fitting one-legged tracksuits and sporting long, brightly painted fingernails. But her appearance took a back seat to her speed, which earned her a silver medal. 1988 proved to be an even better year, and she took home three gold medals and a silver medal, earning the title of "Female Athlete of the Year" by the Associated Press.

Sadly, Joyner passed away in her sleep in 1998 at only 38 years old, after suffering an epileptic seizure. She still holds world records—10.49 seconds and 21.34 seconds—in the 100- and 200-meter events.

(Top right) A Paraguay stamp featuring Florence Griffith Joyner, 1989

(Bottom right) Joyner is greeted by President Ronald Reagan in the Oval Office after the 1988 Olympics.

Tammy Duckworth

Born in Bangkok, Thailand, on March 12, 1968, Tammy Duckworth spent most of her younger years in Southeast Asia, before her family settled in Hawaii when she was 16. She studied political science at the University of Hawaii, and earned a master's degree from George Washington University's Elliot School of International Affairs. Later, she received a PhD in human services from Capella University.

Duckworth became a commissioned officer in the Army Reserve in 1992, where she was trained as a Blackhawk pilot. While deployed in Iraq in 2004, Duckworth's helicopter was hit by a rocket-propelled grenade. As a result of the attack, Duckworth lost both of her legs and much of the use of her right arm. She became an advocate for wounded veterans, and decided to pursue a political career, running for Congress in 2006. Although she lost the race, President Barack Obama later appointed her to a post in the U.S. Department of Veterans Affairs.

In 2012, Duckworth once again ran for Congress and won, becoming the first disabled woman elected to the House of Representatives. She followed that up with a successful run for Senate in 2016—becoming only the second Asian-American woman to serve in the Senate. In 2018, Duckworth achieved another first: She became the first senator to give birth while holding office, when she had her daughter, Maile Pearl.

(Bottom right) Tammy Duckworth walks to the podium during the Democratic National Convention in 2016.

Margaret Chase Smith

Margaret Chase Smith was born in Skowhegan, Maine, on December 14, 1897. After graduating from high school in 1916, she briefly worked as a teacher before joining the staff of her town's weekly newspaper, the *Independent Reporter*. She also became active in local women's organizations, helping to form Skowhegan's chapter of the Business and Professional Women's Club.

In 1930, she married the *Independent Reporter*'s owner, Clyde Smith. Although there was a 21-year age difference between the two, they both shared a love of politics. When Clyde was elected to the House of Representatives in 1936, Smith worked as his secretary, managing his office and becoming familiar with the inner workings of Congress.

After Clyde suffered a heart attack and died in 1940, Smith ran for his seat and won, becoming the first woman from Maine elected to Congress. After eight years in the House, Smith successfully ran for Senate, making her the first woman to serve in both chambers of Congress.

During her tenure, Smith was known as a skilled diplomat and legislator, traveling the world and meeting with the leaders of 23 different nations. She was bestowed with more than 90 honorary degrees in her lifetime, and was awarded the Presidential Medal of Freedom in 1989.

(Top left) Margaret Chase Smith is sworn in to fill the seat of her late husband, Republican Clyde Smith.

Shirley Chisholm

Born to Caribbean immigrants on November 30, 1924, in Brooklyn, New York, Shirley Anita St. Hill spent part of her childhood in Barbados with her grandmother, where she attended a strict, British-style one-room schoolhouse. Back in the U.S. she attended Brooklyn College, and after graduating in 1946 she married Conrad O. Chisholm, a private investigator from Jamaica.

While teaching in a nursery school, Chisholm earned a master's degree in elementary education from Columbia University. She then went on to serve as the director of the Friends Day Nursery in Brooklyn and the Hamilton-Madison Child Care Center in Manhattan, and worked as an educational consultant for the New York City Bureau of Child Welfare.

In the 1960s, Chisholm began taking an interest in politics, doing volunteer work for political clubs and the League of Women Voters, and in 1965 she became a member of the New York State Assembly. In 1968, she was elected to the U.S. House of Representatives, becoming the first black congresswoman. Chisholm used her status to advocate for women and children, helping to create the Special Supplemental Program for Women, Infants, and Children (WIC), and

(Right) A poster for Shirley Chisholm's 1972 presidential campaign

hiring only women to work in her office. She also became one of the founding members of the Congressional Black Caucus and the National Women's Political Caucus.

In January of 1972, Chisholm made history again when she announced a bid for the U.S. presidency, becoming the first woman to run for the Democratic Party's nomination. She was also the first black major-party candidate to run for president. Chisholm struggled to be taken seriously as a presidential candidate, and she lost the nomination to George McGovern. However, Chisholm demonstrated that she was not afraid to shake up the status quo.

Chisholm served seven terms with the House of Representatives, leaving Congress in 1983 and returning to her first love—teaching. She taught politics and sociology at Mount Holyoke College until 1987, and remained active on the lecture circuit. Chisholm, who passed away in 2005 at the age of 80, was posthumously awarded the Presidential Medal of Freedom in 2015.

Nancy Pelosi

Nancy Pelosi was born Nancy Patricia D'Alesandro in Baltimore, Maryland, on March 26, 1940. Her father, Thomas D'Alesandro Jr., was a congressman and the mayor of Baltimore from 1947 to 1959, so it stands to reason that Pelosi became interested in politics at a young age. She attended Trinity College in Washington, D.C., where she graduated with a degree in political science.

After marrying her husband, Paul Pelosi, the couple moved to San Francisco, where Pelosi got her start in politics by volunteering for the Democratic Party. She made a name for herself by campaigning and hosting parties, eventually being elected as a Democratic National Committee member. She also served as party chair for Northern California, and the state Democratic Party.

In 1987, following the death of Representative Sala Galante Burton, Pelosi won a special election to fill her vacancy. As a member of the House of Representatives, she served on the Appropriations Committee and the Permanent Select Committee on Intelligence. Advocating for health care, affordable housing, and human rights, Pelosi emerged as a strong leader of the Democrats in Congress,

and in 2002 she was selected to be the Democratic leader of the House of Representatives—the first woman in history to be chosen for the position.

Four years later, after the 2006 midterm elections flipped control of the House from the Republicans to the Democrats, Pelosi made history again when she was elected Speaker of the House. Not only was she the first woman to hold the Speakership, but as second in line for the presidency after the vice president, Pelosi rose to the highest political position ever held by a woman.

Pelosi was Speaker of the House until 2010, when the Republicans gained control of the House. She has remained minority leader—and a vocal fighter—for her party's values.

Antonia Novello

(Above) Official portrait of Antonia Novello, 14th Surgeon General of the United States

Born in Fajardo, Puerto Rico, on August 23, 1944, Antonia Novello was diagnosed with Hirschsprung's disease—a congenital disorder in which nerves are missing from parts of the intestine—when she was a baby. Novello's struggles with the disease as a child cemented her determination to one day become a doctor.

After graduating from high school at the age of 15, Novello earned a bachelor's degree at the University of Puerto Rico, then received her doctor of medicine from the University of Puerto Rico School of Medicine in 1970. She interned at the University of Michigan Medical School, and later began a residency at Georgetown University School of Medicine Hospital.

In 1979, Novello joined the United States Public Health Service and began working at the National Institutes of Health. She received a commission in the Public Health Service Commissioned Corps, where she was appointed to Assistant Surgeon General in 1986. In 1990, President George H.W. Bush appointed Novello to the position of Surgeon General, making her the first woman and the first Hispanic person to hold the position.

Novello focused on women and children's health, paying specific attention to underage drinking and smoking, as well as pediatric AIDS. She retired in 1993, after receiving numerous medals and awards.

Tammy Baldwin

The first woman to represent Wisconsin in Congress, Tammy Baldwin has lived in the state her whole life. Born on February 11, 1962, in Madison, Baldwin attended Madison West High School where she graduated as valedictorian. She then studied mathematics and government at Smith College before earning a juris doctor from the University of Wisconsin Law School.

By the time she graduated from law school, Baldwin had already begun her political career, serving on the Dane County Board of Supervisors and the Madison Common Council. She was only 24 when she served on the Dane County Board of Supervisors, and she held the position for eight years. She also worked as a lawyer in private practice, until she was elected to the Wisconsin Assembly in 1992, where she was reelected twice.

In 1998, Baldwin made history when she was elected to the U.S. House of Representatives, becoming the first openly gay woman to serve in Congress. A decade later, she was elected to the U.S. Senate. Baldwin was not only the first woman from Wisconsin to serve in the Senate, but also the first openly gay person to serve in the Senate.

(Right) Official portrait of Tammy Baldwin

Hillary Clinton

Hillary Clinton—born Hillary Diane Rodham on October 26, 1947, in Chicago, Illinois—was active in politics at a young age, participating in student council and serving as class vice president her junior year of high school. She attended Wellesley College, where she majored in political science and was active in student government, graduating with honors in 1969.

Moving next to Yale Law School, Clinton worked at the Yale Child Study Center and volunteered free legal services to low-income families. In 1971, she met future husband Bill Clinton—although interestingly, she declined his first (and second, and third) marriage

proposal, unsure of whether she wanted to give up her independence.

When Clinton passed the bar exam in Arkansas, it finally prompted her to say yes to marriage and settling down. But settling down certainly didn't mean slowing down: Clinton taught classes in criminal law at the University of Arkansas, and later worked on Jimmy Carter's presidential campaign. Bill Clinton was elected governor of Arkansas in 1978, and was reelected four times, making Hillary the first lady of the state for a dozen years.

In 1992, Bill Clinton was elected president, and Hillary was once again a first lady. Not one to sit by idly, she became an active, outspoken, and dynamic partner to the president, causing some critics to refer to her as "co-president."

After the presidency, the Clintons bought a home in Chappaqua, New York, and Hillary set her sights on the U.S. Senate, winning a seat and becoming the first woman elected to the Senate from New York. After seven years in the Senate, Clinton announced her intention to run for president, but dropped out when Barack Obama secured the nomination. But Clinton wasn't finished with Washington, D.C.: She became Barack

Obama's Secretary of State in 2009.

Clinton realized her dream of running for president in 2016, becoming the first woman to be on the ticket for a major political party. Although ultimately losing to Donald Trump, Clinton has spent her life shattering glass ceilings, showing women that the hope of a female American president will soon be a reality.

(Top left) Hillary and Bill Clinton campaigning in St. Louis, Missouri, during the 1992 presidential election.

(Bottom right) President Barack Obama and Hillary Clinton at a campaign appearance during the historic 2016 presidential election

Ruth Bader Ginsburg

Ruth Bader Ginsburg was born Joan Ruth Bader on March 15, 1933, in Brooklyn, New York, to working-class parents who emphasized the value of education. She studied government at Cornell University, graduating first in her class in 1954—the same year she married law student Martin D. Ginsburg.

Ginsburg enrolled in Harvard Law School in 1956, where she faced criticism and hostility as one of only nine women in a class of 500 men. The dean of the school even scolded the female students for taking away places in classrooms that could have been filled with male students. But Ginsburg excelled in her classes, becoming the first female member of the Harvard Law Review. When Martin found a job in New York City, she transferred to Columbia University, where she earned a juris doctor degree in 1959, tied for first in her class.

Ginsburg then taught at Rutgers University Law School and at Columbia, where she became the first female tenured professor at the school. She took a great interest in gender equality, serving as director of the Women's Rights Project of the American Civil Liberties Union. Working on their behalf, Ginsburg argued six cases on gender equality before the Supreme Court.

(Left) A photo of Ruth Bader Ginsburg taken in 1977

In 1980, President Jimmy Carter appointed Ginsburg to a seat on the U.S. Court of Appeals for the District of Columbia, where she worked for the next 13 years. In 1993, Ginsburg was nominated as an Associate Justice of the Supreme Court by President Bill Clinton. Seen as a moderate, Ginsburg's confirmation hearings were mostly without controversy, and she was easily confirmed by the Senate with a vote of 96 to 3.

Ginsburg has continued to fight for women's rights and equality during her time on the court, winning the American Bar Association's Thurgood Marshall Award in 1999 for her contributions. Although now in her mid-80s, she has stated that she hopes to remain on the Supreme Court for several more years. Recently, a documentary film about her life, *RBG*, premiered at the 2018 Sundance Film Festival to critical acclaim, introducing a new generation to her inspiring story.

Madeleine Albright

A native of Czechoslovakia, Madeleine Albright was born Maria Jana Korbelova on May 15, 1937, in Prague. Her family fled the country when it was invaded by Nazis at the beginning of World War II, finding temporary refuge in England. Although she was raised a Roman Catholic, Albright would later learn that her parents had converted from Judaism, and that three of her grandparents had died in Nazi concentration camps.

After the war, Albright's family emigrated to the United States, eventually settling in Denver, Colorado. Albright earned a scholarship to Wellesley University, where she graduated with honors in 1959. She then attended Columbia University—while also raising three daughters—and received a PhD in public law and government in 1976.

Albright began a political career working for senator Edward Muskie and for national security advisor Zbigniew Brzezinski during the Carter administration. She then became a professor of international

affairs at Georgetown University, winning the school's Teacher of the Year award four times.

Albright turned back to politics in the late '80s, becoming an advisor to presidential hopeful Michael Dukakis. In 1992, President Bill Clinton appointed her to be the U.S. representative to the United Nations, where she quickly earned a reputation as a tough and assertive advocate of the United States.

In 1996, Clinton nominated Albright for Secretary of State; when she was sworn in on January 23, 1997, she became the first woman to ever hold the position, making her the highest-ranking woman in the history of U.S. government. As Secretary of State, Albright advocated for human rights around the world, fought to stop the spread of nuclear weapons to rogue nations, and helped normalize U.S. relations with countries like Vietnam and China. In 2000, Albright became the first American Secretary of State to travel to North Korea.

Since leaving the position in 2001, Albright has written several books, has launched a private investment fund called Albright Capital Management, and has served on several boards of directors.

(Right) President Barack Obama awards Madeleine Albright the Presidential Medal of Freedom at the White House in 2012.

Diane Humetewa

A member of the Hopi Native American tribe, Diane Humetewa was born in Phoenix, Arizona, on December 5, 1964. She attended Arizona State University, and earned a juris doctor degree from the Sandra Day O'Connor College of Law in 1993.

Seeing the overreach of federal courts into tribal communities, Humetewa wished to raise awareness of issues facing American Indian tribes such as the Hopi. She began her law career as a Tribal Liaison in the office of the United States Attorney for Arizona, where she also served as senior litigation counsel. In 2007, Arizona senators John McCain and John Kyl recommended her as a United States attorney, and on December 17, she was sworn in as a U.S. Attorney for the District of Arizona. Humetewa became the first Native American woman to serve in this role.

In 2013, President Obama nominated Humetewa to serve as a federal district judge in the District of Arizona. She was confirmed unanimously by the Senate, and received her judicial commission on May 14, 2014, becoming the first Native American woman to serve as a federal judge. In a state with a large Native American population, Humetewa's expertise has made her an indispensable advocate for tribal justice.

(Above) Official photo of Diane Humetewa

Esther Peterson

If you ever read nutrition labels to decide which products to buy, you may have Esther Peterson to thank. The daughter of Danish immigrants, Peterson was born on December 9, 1906, in Provo, Utah. After graduating from Brigham Young University, she and her husband, Oliver, moved to Boston, where she volunteered at the local YWCA.

Many of her students worked for the garment industry, and when they went on strike to demand better wages, it inspired Peterson to work with unions. She eventually became a union lobbyist in Washington D.C., where she worked with a then-unknown John F. Kennedy.

When Kennedy became president in 1961, he appointed Peterson head of the Women's Bureau in the Department of Labor, where she advocated for the Equal Pay Act of 1963. By 1964, President Lyndon Johnson chose Peterson to be the Special Assistant for Consumer Affairs, where she spent the next 20 years advocating for truth in advertising, sell-by dates on food packaging, and nutritional labels.

After spending a career fighting for workers' and consumers' rights, Peterson was awarded the Presidential Medal of Freedom in 1981, and was named a UNESCO representative in the United Nations in 1993.

Sally Yates

Born on August 20, 1960, in Atlanta, Georgia, Sally Yates studied journalism at the University of Georgia and earned a juris doctor from the University of Georgia School of Law. She passed the bar exam in 1986, going to work for a law firm specializing in commercial litigation, and three years later was hired as Assistant U.S. Attorney for the Northern District of Georgia.

Yates became known for prosecuting the case of Eric Rudolph, the domestic terrorist who bombed the Centennial Olympic Park in Atlanta during the 1996 Summer Olympics. By 2004, she was Acting U.S. Attorney, working under both Republican and Democratic administrations.

In 2010, Yates was appointed to the position of U.S. Attorney in the Northern District of Georgia by President Obama, becoming the first woman to hold the post. In 2015, the Senate confirmed Yates as the Deputy Attorney General of the United States, where she served under Attorney General Loretta Lynch.

In January 2017, Yates became Acting Attorney General under the Trump administration, but was later dismissed when she refused to defend the controversial Executive Order 13769, which restricted travel to the U.S. from seven Muslim-majority countries. Since then, Yates has returned to private law practice, and frequently lectures at Georgetown University Law Center.

(Left) Official portrait of Deputy Attorney General Sally Yates, 2016

Sonia Sotomayor

Sonia Maria Sotomayor was born on June 25, 1954, in New York City, where she grew up in Spanish-speaking Puerto Rican neighborhoods in the Bronx. A determined child, Sotomayor became fluent in English and, after getting hooked on the *Perry Mason* television series, decided—by the age of ten—that she would one day be a judge.

Sotomayor graduated from Princeton in 1976, then earned a juris doctor from Yale in 1979. After passing the bar exam in 1980, she began her career as an assistant district attorney in Manhattan. In 1984, she entered private practice, making partner by 1988, and began doing pro bono work for agencies like the Puerto Rican Legal Defense and Education Fund. In 1992, President George H.W. Bush nominated her to be a U.S. District Court Judge for the Southern District of New York City, where she became the court's youngest judge. President Clinton then nominated her for the U.S. Second Circuit Court of Appeals.

Earning a reputation as a political centrist, Sotomayor was nominated for Supreme Court Justice by President Obama. When she was confirmed in August 2009, she became the first justice of Hispanic descent on the highest court in the country, far surpassing her childhood dream.

Geraldine Ferraro

Geraldine Anne Ferraro was born on August 26, 1935, in Newburgh, New York, where she attended Marymount Manhattan College at the age of 16 on a scholarship. She then became a teacher, but wanted to pursue a "man's" career instead, so she took night classes at Fordham University to earn a law degree.

Ferraro became an assistant district attorney in Queens County, where she created the special victims bureau to prosecute crimes against children and the elderly. In 1978, she decided to seek political office, running for the House of Representatives for the State of New York. Ferraro won, and immediately earned a reputation as a rising star in the Democratic Party. She focused her attention on women's rights, urging the passage of the Equal Rights Amendment.

Ferraro's work made her a symbol for the feminist movement. When presidential hopeful Walter Mondale chose her to be his running mate in 1984—the first time a woman ran for vice president under either party's ticket—she was met with sizeable crowds of supporters on the campaign trail. Although Reagan and Bush won reelection, Ferraro remained active in politics for the rest of her life, often contributing commentary on CNN and Fox News.

(Left) Geraldine Ferraro at the Democratic National Party Convention in San Francisco, 1984

Patsy Mink

A third-generation descendant of Japanese immigrants—also known as a Sansei—Patsy Matsu Takemoto Mink was born on December 6, 1927, in Paia, on the island of Maui in Hawaii. High school valedictorian, she attended the University of Hawaii at Manoa before transferring to the University of Nebraska. Mink was disturbed by the university's policy of segregation, and she formed a coalition of supporters who successfully campaigned to end the school's segregation policies.

She later returned to the University of Hawaii, earning degrees in zoology and chemistry, then received her juris doctor degree from the University of Chicago Law School. She passed the Hawaii bar exam in 1953, and became the first woman of Japanese descent to practice law in Hawaiian territory. Hawaii became a state in 1959, and Mink took up an interest in politics, serving in the Hawaii State Senate.

(Above) Official portrait of Patsy Mink as a member of the United States House of Representatives

In 1964, Mink became the first Asian-American woman—and the first woman of any ethnic minority—elected to Congress, serving six consecutive terms. Mink focused on equal rights for all, helping to author the revolutionary Title IX. After she passed away in 2002, President George W. Bush renamed Title IX the Patsy T. Mink Equal Opportunity in Education Act, in her honor.

Eleanor Roosevelt

The niece of President Theodore Roosevelt, Anna Eleanor Roosevelt—who preferred to be called by her middle name—was born on October 11, 1884, in New York City. Roosevelt was a shy and serious child, and both of her parents died before she was 10 years old, leaving her depressed and insecure. She was raised by her maternal grandmother and taught by private tutors until she was 15, when she was sent to a private school near London, England. The school helped Roosevelt break out of her shell, and she returned to the United States in 1902 with newfound confidence.

The same year, Roosevelt ran into her father's fifth cousin, Franklin Delano Roosevelt, on a train, and the two began a relationship, becoming engaged in 1903. They married on March 17, 1905, with former President Theodore Roosevelt walking his niece down the aisle.

As Franklin began his political career, Roosevelt became more involved in public service, working for the Red Cross during World War I and campaigning for her husband's run for vice president during the 1920 presidential election. When Franklin was stricken with polio in 1921, some encouraged him to give up his ambitions; but Roosevelt encouraged him to continue, even making appearances on his behalf. Throughout the decade, she made a name for herself as a leader in the Democratic Party, strengthening Franklin's popularity, especially amongst women voters.

FDR took office in 1933, and his wife immediately established herself as a unique First Lady. Not content to stand in the wings, the once-shy Roosevelt

(Left) Eleanor Roosevelt stands with Fala, President Franklin Roosevelt's Scottish terrier.

worked tirelessly for women's rights and children's causes, giving her own press conferences and writing a daily newspaper column. She advocated for Depression-era farmers and coal miners, civil rights, and America's youth, and after the Japanese bombing of Pearl Harbor, she warned against discrimination towards Japanese-Americans. Roosevelt even opposed her husband's order that Japanese-Americans be held in internment camps, for which she was often criticized.

After FDR passed away in 1945, President Truman appointed Roosevelt as a delegate to the United Nations General Assembly, and was reappointed by President Kennedy. In 1968, Roosevelt was posthumously awarded a United Nations Prize in the Field of Human Rights for her work.

(Top left) A statue of Eleanor Roosevelt at the Franklin Delano Roosevelt Memorial in Washington, D.C.

(Bottom right) Eleanor Roosevelt watches a nurse demonstrate a radiation counter at Oak Ridge Cancer Research Hospital in Oak Ridge, Tennessee, 1955.

Condoleezza Rice

Condoleezza Rice was born on November 14, 1954, in Birmingham, Alabama. Her unusual first name is derived from the musical term "con dolcezza," meaning "with sweetness," and as a teenager, Rice intended to live up to her musical name by studying piano and becoming a concert pianist. She initially majored in music at the University of Denver, but then decided to take a different path, graduating with a degree in political science.

After earning a master's degree in political science from Notre Dame University, and a PhD from the Josef Korbel School of International Studies at the University of Denver, Rice joined Stanford University as a professor. She became an expert on the Soviet Union, and in the late-1980s she was asked to work with the United States National

Security Council, advising President George H.W. Bush during the dissolution of the Soviet Union and the reunification of Germany.

In 1993, after returning to her post at Stanford, Rice was appointed provost—the chief academic officer—of the university, becoming the first woman and the first African-American to hold the position. At 39

(Right) Condoleezza Rice shakes hands with South Korean Foreign Minister Ban Ki-moon, 2006.

years old, she was also the youngest provost in the university's history. As provost, she balanced the school's budget, taking it from a deficit of $20 million to a surplus of $14 million in two years.

In 2001, Rice was pulled back into a political career when she was appointed national security advisor by President George W. Bush, earning the nickname "Warrior Princess" for her quiet strength. In 2004, Bush nominated Rice for Secretary of State; when she took office on January 26, 2005, she became the first black woman to hold the post, serving until 2009. As Secretary of State, Rice logged a tiring 1.06 million air miles of travel on diplomatic missions for the Bush administration—a record amount of travel for the position.

Since her time in the White House, Rice has returned to teaching at Stanford, has written several books, and often weighs in on political matters for the media. In 2012 she achieved another first, when she and South Carolina businesswoman Darla Moore became the first women to be admitted to the Augusta National Golf Club in Georgia.

Sandra Day O'Connor

Sandra Day O'Connor was born in El Paso, Texas, on March 26, 1930, and spent much of her childhood on a remote cattle ranch in Arizona, where she became adept at hunting, riding horses, and changing flat tires. The closest school was a 32-mile bus ride away.

After high school, O'Connor studied economics at Stanford University, and then attended the university's law school, graduating third in her class in 1952. Legal jobs for women were scarce at the time, so O'Connor worked for the county attorney of the San Mateo region—without pay—to gain experience. She was soon employed as the deputy county attorney.

After briefly moving overseas when her husband, John Jay O'Connor III, was drafted, the couple eventually

(Top left) Sandra Day O'Connor and President Ronald Reagan sit at the White House, 1981.

(Bottom left) Sandra Day O'Connor is sworn in as a Supreme Court Justice by Justice Warren Burger, 1981.

settled in Maricopa County, Arizona. O'Connor worked in private practice, and then as the state's assistant attorney general, until 1969. When a vacancy opened up in the Arizona Senate, Governor Jack Williams appointed her to the seat; O'Connor then ran for, and won, reelection the following year.

In 1974, she ran for the position of judge in the Maricopa County Superior Court, winning the race. She served until 1979, when she was appointed to the Arizona State Court of Appeals.

During the 1980 presidential campaign, Ronald Reagan vowed to appoint the first woman to the Supreme Court; on August 19, 1981, he delivered on his promise, nominating O'Connor to replace Potter Stewart. On September 21, the Senate voted unanimously to confirm, and she became the first female justice on the Supreme Court.

Within her first year on the court, O'Connor received more than 60,000 letters from the public— most were positive, but a few criticized her presence on the male-dominated court. Drawing on the lessons in tenacity she learned as a child on her family's ranch, O'Connor was determined to prove that a woman could thrive in a man's world. She spent 24 years on the court, retiring in 2006 but staying active on the lecture circuit and writing several books. She was awarded the Presidential Medal of Freedom in 2009.

(Right) A photo of Sandra Day O'Connor taken between 1981 and 1983

Amelia Earhart

Amelia Earhart was born in Atchison, Kansas, in 1897. From a young age, Earhart's mother encouraged young Amelia's sense of adventure. She spent much of her time playing outside, collecting bugs, and hunting rats. Throughout her childhood, she compiled a scrapbook of newspaper clippings on women in male-oriented fields. Earhart was homeschooled with her sister until the family moved to Des Moines, Iowa, and the children enrolled in public school.

The family relocated to Minnesota, Missouri, and finally Chicago, where Earhart finished her senior year of high school. After briefly attending college in Pennsylvania, Earhart moved to Toronto and served as a nurse to soldiers during World War I. She then moved

(Above) Amelia Earhart stands in front of the Lockheed Electra, the plane she was flying when she disappeared in 1937.

to California to live with her parents.

In 1920, Earhart took a 10-minute plane ride while visiting an airfield, and she decided that she wanted to learn how to fly. She saved up $1,000 for flying lessons, and eventually bought her own biplane. She was the 16th woman in the U.S. to be issued a pilot's license.

In the 1920s, Earhart's family lost their money, and her parents got divorced. She moved to Boston with her mother and found employment as a teacher and a social worker. While in Massachusetts, Earhart con-

(Left) Amelia Earhart and the sports plane she bought in 1928

(Top right) Earhart is cheered by admirers after becoming the first woman to complete a solo Atlantic flight, 1932.

tinued to show an interest in flying, becoming the vice president of the American Aeronautical Society's Boston Chapter and investing in a local airport, which she also flew out of.

In 1928, Earhart got an offer to be the first woman to fly across the Atlantic Ocean. Wilmer Stultz acted as the pilot and Louis Gordon the copilot on the 20-hour trip, and Earhart kept a flight log. Stultz, Gordon, and Earhart were celebrated as heroes upon their return to the United States, and Earhart eventually gained celebrity status.

In 1932, Earhart became the first woman to fly solo nonstop across the Atlantic Ocean. She continued making solo flights to and from different destinations, and set seven women's aviation records between 1930 and 1935.

In 1937, Earhart began the first around-the-world-flight at the equator. After completing over 22,000 miles of her flight, she and her navigator vanished. A search effort went on for weeks, but Earhart and her navigator were never found.

(Bottom right) Amelia Earhart sits in the cockpit of the Lockheed Electra airplane.

Tarana Burke

After sexual harassment claims against Hollywood producer Harvey Weinstein came to light in 2017, the Me Too movement spread like wildfire; but the origins of the famous two-word phrase began more than a decade earlier. The phrase was coined by Tarana Burke—born on September 12, 1973, in the Bronx—who began using it on a Myspace social media page in 2006 to draw attention to issues of sexual abuse and harassment.

After graduating from Auburn University, Burke settled in Selma, Alabama, where she began working with victims of sexual assault. She founded the nonprofit organization Just Be Inc. in 2003, which focused on the wellbeing of young women of color. Often struggling to find words of comfort for the girls who shared their stories with her, Burke—a survivor of abuse herself—simply began to tell them that they were not alone, by saying "this happened to me too."

The short phrase became a way for Burke to assure other survivors that they were heard and understood. After the Weinstein abuse allegations, the #MeToo hashtag took on a new life, taking social media by storm and making Burke—along with other female activists—*Time* magazine's Person of the Year.

(Left) Tarana Burke at the 2018 Time *100 Gala*

Winona LaDuke

Winona LaDuke was born on August 18, 1959, in Los Angeles, California, to a mother of European Jewish ancestry and a father of Native American Ojibwe descent, from the White Earth Indian Reservation in Minnesota. Her father's advocacy for the Ojibwe people greatly influenced LaDuke as child, and at 18, she spoke at the United Nations about Native American issues—the youngest person to ever do so.

LaDuke earned an economics degree from Harvard, and in 1982 moved to White Earth to be the principal of a reservation high school. Living on the reservation for the first time, LaDuke was more aware of the injustices faced by indigenous peoples, and in 1989 she founded the White Earth Land Recovery Project, which aimed to restore and preserve the land and traditional practices of the Ojibwe. The project has helped to return at least 1,400 acres of land to native peoples.

Hoping to further increase awareness of native environmental issues, LaDuke founded Honor the Earth in 1993. The non-profit uses music, art, and media to raise funds and support for indigenous environmental issues, such as the Dakota Access Pipeline controversy.

In addition to her activism, LaDuke has also been a vice-presidential candidate, running with Ralph Nader on the Green Party ticket in 1996 and 2000.

(Above) A photo of Winona LaDuke taken in the 1970s

Helen Keller

Born on June 27, 1880, in Tuscumbia, Alabama, Helen Keller was a healthy baby who started talking at only six months old. But when she was 19 months old, Keller contracted what her doctor called "brain fever"—most probably either scarlet fever or meningitis—which left her both blind and deaf. Throughout her childhood, she developed her own gestures to communicate with her family; but she was also often unruly and angry, venting frustrations through tantrums, leading some family members to suggest she should be institutionalized.

Desperate to give her daughter a better life, Keller's mother searched for help, eventually contacting the Perkins Institute for the Blind, which sent former student Anne Sullivan to instruct Keller. Although a frustrating endeavor at first, within a month Keller was able to recognize the signs for "water" that Sullivan made into the palm of her hand, suddenly understanding the connection between signs and objects.

(Above) Helen Keller, age 8, sits with her teacher, Anne Sullivan, 1888.

With more understanding of the world around her, Keller began formal education, attending the Perkins Institute, the Wright-Humason School for the Deaf, and Horace Mann School for the Deaf, where she painstakingly learned how to speak. In 1900, she was admitted to Radcliffe College, the women's college of Harvard University, where Sullivan sat next to her in classes to interpret lectures. Keller graduated in 1904 as the first blind-deaf person to earn a bachelor's degree.

After college, Keller's story spread throughout the country, and she used her fame to advocate for social issues, even testifying before Congress to lobby for improved welfare for the blind. In 1920 she helped to found the American Civil Liberties Union, and she often participated in campaigns to raise awareness and funds for people with disabilities. By 1957, Keller had travelled to 35 countries, sharing encouragement and inspiration with the world. Throughout her remarkable life, Keller published 12 books, was awarded several honorary doctoral degrees, was elected to the Women's Hall of Fame, and received the Presidential Medal of Freedom.

Jane Addams

As a child, Jane Addams—born on September 6, 1860, in Cedarville, Illnois—loved to read, especially the works of Charles Dickens. The author's stories featuring characters struggling with their lower-class social conditions inspired the young Addams to dream of one day working with and helping the poor. She attended Rockford Female Seminary, graduating in 1881, and then moved to Philadelphia to study medicine at the Women's Medical College of Philadelphia.

Unfortunately, Addams was plagued with health issues and she was forced to drop out of school, depressed that her dream to help others was dashed. But after a trip to London with a friend, Addams visited Toynbee Hall—a settlement house created to help the poor—and realized she could still help the less fortunate, medical degree or not.

Addams grew determined to create a place like Toynbee Hall in the United States; and in 1889, she and friend Ellen Gates Starr co-founded Hull House in Chicago. The settlement house provided services to immigrants and the poor living in the city, and soon 2,000 people a week were making use of its facilities. Hull House expanded to encompass 13 buildings, and included a night school for adults, art classes, child care, a public kitchen, apartments, and many other social programs.

Always emphasizing the importance of caring for children, Addams began serving on Chicago's Board of Education in 1905. The same year, she became a charter member of the American Sociological

(Above) A photo of Jane Addams from either 1924 or 1926

(Left) Jane Addams speaks to a crowd, 1915.

(Below) A photo of Jane Addams in a car, taken in 1915

Society, and in 1910 was named the first female president of the National Conference of Charities and Corrections.

"The mother of social work," as she became known, was also a committed pacifist, who often gave lectures on her ideas for ending war in the world. After World War I began, Addams became chair of the Women's Peace Party and served as president of the Women's International League for Peace and Freedom until 1929. For her efforts, she was awarded the Nobel Peace Prize in 1931—the first American woman to win the award.

Adena Friedman

In 2015, Adena Friedman—born in Baltimore, Maryland, in 1969—was listed just behind Nancy Pelosi in *Forbes*' list of the 40 most powerful women in the world. Freidman, who attended an all-girls school for ten years before heading to college, partially credits her female-friendly education for propelling her to such a status. With no boys in the classroom, Friedman and her classmates felt free to ask questions and embrace traditionally "male" subjects like science and math.

While studying in the co-ed environment of Williams College, Friedman noticed that the women in her classes were less vocal than they had been in her early school experiences, and she vowed to always speak up and ask questions. She went on to earn an MBA from Vanderbilt University's Owen Graduate School of Management, and then immediately began working as a business analyst for NASDAQ.

Friedman worked her way up through the ranks of the company, and on January 1, 2017, her determination to be seen as an equal with her male counterparts paid off when she took the position of NASDAQ CEO—making her the first woman to lead a global stock exchange company.

(Left) An electronic board in New York City's Times Square shows a NASDAQ quotation, 2018.

Madam C.J. Walker

Sarah Breedlove—better known as Madam C.J. Walker—was born on December 23, 1867, in Delta, Louisiana. Orphaned at seven, married at 14, and widowed by 20, Walker's younger years were full of struggle and hardship. She moved to St. Louis in 1888 to be closer to her brothers, who worked as barbers.

Ironically, Walker herself was plagued with skin and scalp issues, causing her to lose much of her hair. Not wanting to irritate her skin further with the lye soaps that were common in the day, Walker began to develop her own line of hair care products.

In 1905, she moved to Denver, Colorado, and began selling her new hair care products using the catchy "Madam C.J. Walker" name to market them. They became wildly popular, and Walker was eventually able to expand her operation to include a factory, laboratory, salon, and a school to train sales agents, known as "Walker Agents."

When Walker passed away in 1919, her estate was worth about $600,000—at a time when an average yearly salary was $750—and her business was worth $1 million. By today's dollars, Walker was worth around $8 million, making her one of the first American women to become a self-made millionaire. She is still considered one of the most successful African American business owners ever.

(Left) A portrait of Madam C.J. Walker, taken between 1905 and 1919

Margaret Sanger

Margaret Sanger was born Margaret Louise Higgins on September 14, 1879, in Corning, New York. She attended Claverack College and the Hudson River Institute, then studied nursing at White Plains Hospital. In 1902, she married architect William Sanger, and the couple and their three children eventually settled in Greenwich Village in New York City.

In the bohemian neighborhood, Sanger began to embrace feminism, and in 1912 wrote a series of scandalous (for the day) columns on sex education for the magazine *New York Call*. She also began working as a nurse in the slums on the East Side, frequently meeting women who had undergone back-alley abortions or attempted to self-terminate pregnancies, and Sanger was dismayed that these women had no access to contraception.

In 1914, Sanger began publishing a magazine called *The Woman Rebel*, which advocated for a woman's right to birth control; however, the information she provided was considered "obscene and immoral," and her distribution of the magazine was illegal. Sanger fled to England to avoid prosecution, returning to the U.S. after charges against her were dropped. But she didn't come back alone: Sanger smuggled diaphragms back into the country.

In 1916, Sanger opened a birth control clinic in Brooklyn—distributing some of the contraband diaphragms—and was arrested nine days later. But she scored a win when a court ultimately decided to allow doctors to prescribe birth control for medical reasons. Her case drew attention across the country, increasing support for legal birth control.

Sanger founded the American Birth Control League in 1921, a precursor to the Planned Parenthood Federation of America. Her continued efforts led to a 1936 court ruling that made it legal to import contraceptive devices into the country, and she was instrumental in recruiting biologist Gregory Pincus to develop the first oral contraceptive.

(Above) While seated at a desk, Margaret Sanger is surrounded by 12 other women. This photo was taken in 1920.

(Right) Photo taken in 1916 of the Sanger Clinic on Amber Street in Brooklyn, New York

Clara Barton

Born on Christmas Day, 1821, in North Oxford, Massachusetts, Clara Barton was an extremely shy child who often preferred reading to socializing. But after her brother David was injured in a fall, she took it upon herself to nurse him back to health, and discovered that she enjoyed helping people. Her parents encouraged her to become to teacher, hoping she could overcome her shyness and put her desire to help others to good use.

Barton began teaching at only 16 years old, working for more than a decade, eventually opening the first free public school in New Jersey. She then moved to Washington, D.C. and worked as a clerk in the U.S. Patent Office.

When the Civil War broke out, Barton's helpful nature once again kicked in, and she vowed to assist in any way she could. She collected and distributed supplies for the soldiers, at first using her own home as a storage area. As word spread, donations of supplies, food, and clothing began pouring in, and Barton began working on the front lines, distributing donations and tending to wounded soldiers—both Union and Confederate. For her work, she became known as the "American Nightingale" and the "Angel of the Battlefield."

After the war, Barton traveled to Europe and worked with a relief organization known as the International Red Cross. Impressed with the work of the group, she lobbied for an American counterpart when she returned to the U.S. In 1881, the American Red Cross was established—headed by Barton—and immediately began providing assistance to victims of floods, famines, and other crises.

Although Barton passed away in 1912, she left behind a familiar legacy: The red cross on a white background is now one of the most recognizable symbols in the country.

(Right) A portrait of Clara Barton, taken circa 1906

Michelle Obama

Growing up, Michelle Obama—born Michelle LaVaughn Robinson on January 17, 1964, in Chicago, Illinois—was a hardworking, gifted student, who graduated salutatorian of her high school class. She then studied sociology at Princeton University, and earned a juris doctor from Harvard Law School in 1988.

While beginning her law career at the firm of Sidley Austin LLP in Chicago, she met Barack Obama, who was interning at the same firm. The two married in 1992, eventually welcoming daughters Malia and Sasha, and the family settled in the Hyde Park neighborhood of Chicago.

Meanwhile, Obama left her corporate job and decided to switch her career to public service, working as an assistant to the mayor and heading up a nonprofit. In 2005, she was appointed vice president for community and external affairs for the University of Chicago Hospitals.

In 2007, Obama greatly reduced her professional responsibilities to campaign with her husband—then a U.S.

(Top right) Michelle Obama stands with Barack Obama and daughters Malia and Sasha on November 4, 2008, just after Barack Obama was elected president.

Senator—during the run for the Democratic presidential nomination. Barack Obama was inaugurated as president on January 20, 2009, making Obama the first African-American first lady in United States history.

During the president's two terms, Obama was an advocate for women, children, the homeless, and military families, twice being awarded the Jerald Washington Memorial Founders' Award by the National Coalition for Homeless Veterans.

But perhaps Obama's greatest passion was her commitment to healthy eating and ending childhood obesity. She created the "Let's Move!" initiative to encourage kids to make healthy food choices and to try

new sports and activities. She also instructed the White House kitchen to prepare organic food for all guests, and planted a 1,100-square-foot vegetable garden on the South Lawn.

Since leaving the White House, Obama has continued her fight for a healthier America and is frequently invited to speak on many topics.

(Above) Michelle Obama in Los Angeles, California, helps with Barack Obama's 2008 preidential compaign.

(Left) First Lady Michelle Obama stands with presidential candidate Hillary Clinton during her 2016 presidential campaign.

Bessie Coleman

(Above) Bessie Coleman stands on the wheel of her plane, 1922.

Born in Atlanta, Texas, on January 26, 1892, Bessie Coleman and her family moved to Waxahachie when she was two. At six she began attending school, walking four miles every day to reach a segregated, one-room schoolhouse, where she excelled at reading and math.

In 1916, Coleman moved to Chicago, Illinois, where she worked as a manicurist in a barbershop. When she heard stories from the World War I pilots frequenting the shop, Coleman knew she wanted to fly. But as a woman and the daughter of an African-American mother and a mostly Cherokee father, she was denied entry to American flight schools. So Coleman took a proactive approach: She took classes in French, then moved to Paris, where she learned to fly.

Coleman became the first woman of African-American and Native American descent to earn a pilot's license and an international aviation license. She returned to the U.S. and became a hugely popular stunt flyer and parachutist, admired by both people of all races for her daring aerial maneuvers.

Sadly, Coleman died at the young age of 34, after an accident during a stunt rehearsal. She was inducted into the National Aviation Hall of Fame in 2006, still an inspiration to women in aviation.

Wendy Kopp

Wendy Kopp was born on June 29, 1967, in Austin, Texas. She attended Princeton University, where she majored in public policy in the Woodrow Wilson School of Public and International Affairs. While in college, Kopp encountered students from a diverse array of backgrounds, and she became aware that those from disadvantaged areas were less prepared for college than those from more affluent areas. This sparked an idea for her senior thesis, where she proposed an idea for improving the American system of education.

Kopp's idea was to create an organization modeled on the Peace Corps that would recruit recent college graduates to teach in poorly served urban and rural areas. Kopp's idea— with the help of donors including Ross Perot—became a reality when she founded Teach for America in 1990, with 500 recent graduates serving as the charter corps members. Success was immediate, and donations for the organization began pouring in.

By 2013, more than 10,000 Teach for America members were teaching in the country's neediest communities, and Kopp had also created Teach for All, a global network of teachers for communities around the world. Kopp has received numerous awards for her work, including honorary doctorates from Harvard, Boston University, and her alma mater, Princeton.

(Above) Wendy Kopp speaks at the World Economic Forum in Davos, Switzerland, 2012.

Margaret Fuller

Sarah Margaret Fuller was born on May 23, 1810, in Cambridgeport, Massachusetts. Her father, Congressman Timothy Fuller, taught her to read and write when she was only three years old, providing her with the kind of strict education only available to boys of the time. She began her formal education in 1819, attending several girls' schools, but at age 16 returned home, where she taught herself several languages and read classic literature.

When her father died of cholera in 1835, a distraught Fuller took on the responsibility of caring for her widowed mother and younger siblings. She found teaching jobs, first in Boston then in Providence, Rhode Island, and in 1840 moved her family to Jamaica Plain, Massachusetts. It was here that she began holding her "conversations"—discussions between local women on everything from art and literature to women's rights.

After a trip through the Midwest in 1843, Fuller published her first book, *Summer on the Lakes*. She used the library at Harvard College for research, becoming the first woman given permission to use the Harvard library. In 1945 she published what is considered the first major feminist work in the U.S., *Woman in the Nineteenth Century*.

Fuller's reputation as a well-read intellectual prompted even men of the era to take her seriously, and she advocated for women's rights and social reform throughout her life.

(Top right) A print of Margaret Fuller from 1872

(Bottom right) A copy of the only known daguerreotype of Margaret Fuller, dating back to the early 1850s

Edith Wharton

The daughter of a prestigious New York City family, Edith Newbold Jones—who would later marry Edward Robbins Wharton—was born on January 24, 1862. Her wealthy family traveled extensively when she was a child, and their well-to-do lifestyle is said to have spawned the phrase, "keeping up with the Joneses." Still, Wharton eschewed the etiquette expected of proper ladies of the time, preferring to study books and foreign languages rather than attending fancy parties.

Wharton began a writing career at the age of 15. Between 1877 and 1880, she published poems and novellas anonymously or under pseudonyms; her family disapproved of her occupation, considering it inappropriate for a woman. Discouraged by the lack of support, Wharton did not publish anything for nine more years.

But by the late 1800s, Wharton began writing again in earnest. An avid gardener and interior designer, her first major published work was 1897's *The Decoration of Houses*. Wharton loved design so much that she designed her own house, The Mount, which still stands in Lenox, Massachusetts.

Wharton's greatest success would be her 1920 novel *The Age of Innocence*, which made her the first woman to win the Pulitzer Prize for literature. In all, Wharton wrote 15 novels, seven novellas, 85 short stories, and numerous non-fiction works.

Julia Ward Howe

Born on May 27, 1819, in New York City, Julia Ward Howe was a well-read child who grew up around the likes of Charles Dickens, Charles Sumner, and fellow social activist Margaret Fuller. After her father died in 1849, she moved to Boston, where she met and eventually married Samuel Gridley Howe. The couple had six children, but Howe was frequently unhappy in her marriage, wishing to have greater freedom but constrained by her husband, who rigidly believed women should be at home.

Still, Howe was able to pursue her love of writing, publishing essays and a book of poetry, *Passion Flowers*, without her husband's knowledge. When her work as a published author caught his attention, it became a source of trouble in their marriage, especially since many of Howe's published works criticized traditional women's roles and marriage.

Howe's best-known work, however, was written after she and her husband visited Washington, D.C. during the Civil War. Howe noticed the soldiers singing a marching song called "John Brown's Body," and decided to write some new lyrics for the tune. Her poem became the "Battle Hymn of the Republic", which was published in the *Atlantic Monthly* in 1862 and became a rallying cry not only for the Civil War, but for the abolitionists and suffrage movements.

Harper Lee

Born in the racially divided Monroeville, Alabama, on April 28, 1926, Nelle Harper Lee is best known for her 1960 novel *To Kill a Mockingbird*, which contains details from Lee's own life. Just like the book's protagonist—Scout Finch—Lee grew up as a tomboy. When she was a child, her father, a lawyer, defended two black men on trial for murdering a white storekeeper. Lee's father lost the case, resulting in the death penalty for both his clients. This incident shaped the story in her classic novel.

Lee always loved writing, and had an interest in English literature. While in college at the University of Alabama at Tuscaloosa, she wrote for the school's newspaper and humor magazine, but temporarily put her writing aside when she was accepted into law school. It was soon apparent that law was not her passion, however, and she dropped out to return to writing, moving to New York City in 1949 to pursue her dream.

For years, Lee struggled to support herself; but in 1956, her friend, Broadway composer Michael Martin Brown, offered to supplement her income for a year so she could write full time. A grateful Lee dove into her manuscript, which became *To Kill a Mockingbird*. The book won the Pulitzer Prize, has been translated into 40 languages, and continues to sell more than a million copies a year.

(Right) President George Bush awards Harper Lee the Presidential Medal of Freedom in 2007.

Katie Couric

Katherine Anne Couric was born on January 7, 1957, in Arlington, Virginia. She became interested in journalism at an early age, interning at the all-news radio station WAVA in Washington, D.C., while she was in high school and working at *The Cavalier Daily* newspaper while enrolled at the University of Virginia.

After earning her degree in American Studies, Couric landed her first job as a desk assistant at ABC, where she worked with anchorman Sam Donaldson. Soon after, she joined CNN as an assignment editor, and worked for WTVJ in Miami, Florida, and WRC-TV in Washington, D.C.

In 1989, with her career taking off, Couric began working as a reporter at the Pentagon, covering the U.S. invasion of Panama and the Persian Gulf War. She also began filling in for hosts on NBC's morning show, *Today*, and became a permanent co-host in 1991. She remained on the show for 15 years, until May 31, 2006. On September 5 of that year, Couric made her debut on the *CBS Evening News with Katie Couric*, becoming the first woman to anchor the program solo. She also contributed to *60 Minutes* and anchored primetime news specials, earning a salary of $15 million a year—a number that made her the highest paid journalist in the world.

(Left) Katie Couric on stage at the NBC Today Show Concert Series in 2005

In addition to her professional fame, Couric's personal life made headlines in 1998 after her husband, 42-year-old legal analyst Jay Monahan, died of colon cancer. Couric made it her mission to raise awareness of the disease, even undergoing an on-air colonoscopy. Her efforts helped to raise more than $10 million for research.

Although her first love is journalism, Couric has also written several children's books, including *The Brand New Kid*—which topped the *New York Times* best-seller list for three weeks—and *The Blue Ribbon Day*. It seems that anything this journalist, anchor, and writer sets her mind to, she can accomplish.

(Below) Katie Couric hosts the 63rd Annual Peabody Awards in 2004.

Louisa May Alcott

Growing up with family friends like Ralph Waldo Emerson and Henry David Thoreau, Louisa May Alcott may have been destined to be a writer. Born on November 29, 1832, in Germantown, Pennsylvania, she was taught mostly by her father and her literary neighbors; but at a young age she was forced to find work to help support her poverty-stricken family. Writing became a form of escape for Alcott, and in 1849 she finished her first book, *Flower Fables*.

By 1851, Alcott was regularly publishing poems and stories under the pen names Flora Fairfield and A. M. Barnard. After a stint as a hospital nurse during the Civil War, Alcott decided to pursue writing more seriously, publishing essays about her experiences during the war in the *Atlantic Monthly* under her real name, and becoming the editor of a girls' magazine called *Merry's Museum*.

But it was the success of her most famous novel, *Little Women*—which Alcott wrote in two parts published in 1868 and 1869—that ensured her fame in the literary world. The book contains many autobiographical details of Alcott's life with her three sisters, Anna, Elizabeth, and Abigail. Alcott based the novel's heroine, Jo, on herself.

A staunch feminist throughout her life, Alcott ignored the social norms of the time that suggested women must marry in order to be financially stable. The publication of *Little Women* provided her with financial independence and a steady career.

Although Little Women's Jo marries at the end of the novel, Alcott herself remained unmarried throughout her life, instead focusing on her work, regularly publishing stories, novels, and poems. Her books include *Little Men* and *Jo's Boys*, which continued the story of *Little Women*, as well as *Eight Cousins* and *Under the Lilacs*.

Alcott passed away on March 6, 1888, after suffering a stroke. She was buried in Sleepy Hollow Cemetery in Concord, Massachusetts, near family friends Emerson and Thoreau.

(Opposite page) Orchard House, the historic home of Louisa May Alcott and her family, is now a museum. The house is located in Concord, Massachusetts.

(Direct right) A photo of Louisa May Alcott at age 20

Ida Tarbell

Ida Minerva Tarbell was born in a log cabin home in Erie County, Pennsylvania, on November 5, during the financial Panic of 1857. Her family struggled until the Pennsylvania oil rush began in 1859. But the oil business Tarbell's father began was one of many small businesses affected by the South Improvement Company scheme in 1872, which sought to secretly make deals between railroads and large oil companies. Tarbell's experiences with the oil industry would go on to affect the rest of her life.

In 1880, Tarbell was the only woman in her graduating class at Allegheny College. She began a teaching career, but soon left it to pursue writing. She was offered a job at the journal *The Chautauquan*, and later worked at *McClure's Magazine*, where she wrote popular pieces on Napoleon Bonaparte and Abraham Lincoln.

But her most significant work was an investigative piece called *The History of the Standard Oil Company*, which she wrote in 19 installments that were published in *McClure's*. Tarbell exposed Standard's questionable practices, like those that affected her father years earlier. Her work became instrumental in breaking up the oil giant's monopoly, and even led to the creation of the Federal Trade Commission.

(Left) A photo of Ida Tarbell taken between 1910 and 1920, after her years at McClure's

Betty Friedan

Born Bettye Naomi Goldstein on February 4, 1921, in Peoria, Illinois, Betty Friedan began writing as a teenager, when she and a group of friends at Peoria High School created their own literary magazine called *Tide*. While attending Smith College, she became editor-in-chief of the college newspaper, where her political writings often stirred up controversy on campus.

After college, Friedan became a journalist writing for *The Federated Press* and labor union publications, but after becoming pregnant with her second child, she lost her job. Although she wrote some freelance articles for publications including *Cosmopolitan*, Friedan mostly focused on staying home to raise her children, even though she felt unfulfilled in this role.

Wondering if other women felt the same, Friedan embarked on a survey of college graduates and discovered that many housewives felt depressed and dissatisfied with their lives. She used her findings to write her 1963 book, *The Feminine Mystique*, which encouraged women to seek out the opportunities and careers they desired. The book became a bestseller, and has often been credited for beginning the "second wave" of feminism in the United States.

Friedan went on to co-found the National Organization for Women and became its first president, where she lobbied to outlaw discrimination in the workplace and for equal pay for the sexes.

(Below right) Betty Friedan in her home, photographed between 1978 and 1981 by Lynn Gilbert. Copies of The Feminine Mystique *and her 1976 book* It Changed My Life *sit on the coffee table.*

Maya Angelou

Maya Angelou—born Marguerite Annie Johnson on April 4, 1928, in St. Louis, Missouri—had a difficult and horrific childhood. After her parents split up when she was three years old, Angelou and her older brother, Bailey, were shuffled between living with their grandmother and their mother for the next decade. During one of her visits with her mother, when Angelou was only eight years old,

she was molested and raped by her mother's boyfriend. Although the boyfriend was convicted of the crime, he spent a mere day in prison; to exact vengeance, Angelou's uncles found the offender and killed him.

The experience was so traumatic that Angelou stopped speaking for five years. In her young mind, she believed she was responsible for the man's murder because she spoke up and identified him. She stated, "I thought I would never speak again, because my voice would kill anyone."

But a family friend soon introduced Angelou to writers like Charles Dickens, William Shakespeare, and Edgar Allan Poe, as well as black

(Above) Maya Angelou stands with fellow North Carolina Award recipients in 1987.

President Barack Obama presents Maya Angelou with the Presidential Medal of Freedom in 2011.

A photo of Maya Angelou on display at the "Taste of Soul" luncheon in England to kick off Black History Month, February 2014.

Maya Angelou recites her poem "On the Pulse of Morning" at Bill Clinton's inauguration in 1993.

female writers like Jessie Redmon Fauset and Anne Spencer. Angelou quickly developed a love of literature and creativity. Her voice returned, and she began singing, dancing, and acting, appearing in off-Broadway plays and releasing an album, *Miss Calypso*.

In the 1960s, Angelou spent time living in Egypt and Ghana, and when she returned to the U.S. she was active in the civil rights movement, befriending both Malcolm X and Dr. Martin Luther King Jr. Devastated after the leaders were assassinated, Angelou threw herself into creative work, publishing her most famous book, the autobiography *I Know Why the Caged Bird Sings*, in 1969. In 1971, her collection of poetry, *Just Give Me a Cool Drink of Water 'Fore I Die*, was nominated for the Pulitzer Prize.

In addition to writing, Angelou acted in the TV miniseries *Roots*, and films like *How to Make an American Quilt* and *Madea's Family Reunion*, and directed the 1998 film *Down in the Delta*. The prolific artist passed away on May 28, 2014, with President Barack Obama calling her "a brilliant writer, a fierce friend, and a truly phenomenal woman."

Nora Ephron

It's not a stretch to say that Nora Ephron and romantic comedies go hand in hand. The filmmaker, born on May 19, 1941, in New York City, is best known for films like *Sleepless in Seattle* and *You've Got Mail*. The daughter of playwrights, Ephron was named after the main protagonist in Henrik Ibsen's play *A Doll's House*; with such literary beginnings, is it any wonder she went on to create some of film's most beloved characters?

Before filmmaking, however, Ephron worked as a journalist, reporting for the *New York Post* and frequently contributing to *Esquire* magazine. In 1979, while pregnant with her second child, Ephron discovered her husband was having an affair. This prompted her to write her first novel, *Heartburn*, published in 1982, which was later made into a film starring Meryl Streep and Jack Nicholson. Soon after writing her book, she launched her screenwriting career with the script for the film *Silkwood*, which she cowrote with Alice Arlen. The duo was nominated for an Oscar for their work.

But it was Ephron's next screenplay, for the hit *When Harry Met Sally*, that elevated her fame in Hollywood. Filmgoers immediately fell in love with the title characters, and the movie has become a classic example of a romantic comedy.

(Right) Nora Ephron at a special screening of Julie and Julia *in Los Angeles, 2009*

Gwendolyn Brooks

Although she was born in Topeka, Kansas, on June 7, 1917, Gwendolyn Elizabeth Brooks always considered Chicago—where her family moved when she was only six weeks old—her true home. She began writing at an early age, publishing her first poem at the age of 13, and publishing an impressive 75 poems over the next few years.

Brooks began participating in poetry workshops, earning an award from the Midwestern Writers' Conference in 1943. While working as a secretary to support herself, she published her first book of poetry, *A Street in Bronzeville*, in 1945. The book, which provided a glimpse into the poet's South Side Chicago neighborhood, was immediately praised by critics. Brooks earned a Guggenheim Fellowship, and was hailed as one of "Ten Young Women of the Year" in *Mademoiselle* magazine.

Continuing to explore the experiences of growing up in Chicago, Brooks published her second book of poetry, *Annie Allen*, in 1949. The book, which follows the life of a black girl as she grows up in Bronzeville, won a Pulitzer Prize, making Brooks the first African-American to win the prize.

Brooks had a desire to share her love of poetry with others, and spent much of her career teaching—not only in her beloved Chicago, but in colleges and universities around the country.

(Right) A bronze bust of Gwendolyn Brooks located in Washington, D.C.

Barbara Walters

Born on September 25, 1929, in Boston, Massachusetts, Barbara Walters is now one of the most well-known names in journalism. Her family bounced around between Boston, New York, and Miami when she was young, eventually settling in New York, where Walters went to high school. She then earned an English degree from Sarah Lawrence College in 1951.

Almost immediately, she found work at New York City's NBC affiliate, WNBT-TV, where she did publicity and wrote press releases. After leaving NBC, she became a writer for *The Morning Show* on CBS. In 1961, Walters returned to NBC as a writer for the popular *Today* show, where she was mostly tasked with reporting on lighter "women's" stories. Not content to be, as she called it, a "tea pourer," Walters lobbied to take on more serious news reports, including an assignment to India and Pakistan with First Lady Jacqueline Kennedy.

Walters remained on *The Today Show* for 11 years, proving herself to be a serious journalist, and was even chosen to be part of the press corps on President Richard Nixon's historic visit to China.

(Top right) Barbara Walters interviews President Gerald Ford and First Lady Betty Ford at the White House in 1976.

(Bottom right) Barbara Walters sits with President Jimmy Carter and First Lady Rosalynn Carter during an interview in 1978.

In 1976, she became the first woman to co-anchor an evening news program when she joined the *ABC Evening News*. In 1979, she and her former *Today* colleague Hugh Downs began working on the newsmagazine show *20/20*, which Walters went on to co-host for the next 25 years.

During her career, Walters has scored some impressive interviews, including exclusive interviews with leaders like former President Richard Nixon, Cuba's Fidel Castro, and Libya's Muammar al-Gaddafi, and celebrities like Michael Jackson, Katherine Hepburn, and Sir Laurence Olivier. Her 1999 interview of Monica Lewinsky was seen by a record-breaking 74 million viewers—the highest rating ever for a news program—and she was the first journalist to interview actor Christopher Reeve after his devastating horseback-riding accident that left him paralyzed.

More recently, Walters was co-creator, co-producer, and co-host on the daytime talk show *The View*. Although she announced her retirement from television journalism in 2013, she has occasionally come out of retirement to host *20/20* specials and news interviews, with her last on-air interview featuring then-presidential candidate Donald Trump.

(Above left) Barbara Walters at a book signing of her book Audition *in 2008*

(Above right) Barbara Walters is honored with a star on the Hollywood Walk of Fame in 2007.

Gloria Steinem

Born on March 25, 1934, in Toledo, Ohio, Gloria Marie Steinem's childhood would shape the rest of her life. Her father was a traveling salesman who moved his family around the country throughout each year, and her mother was stricken with mental illness. When Steinem was ten years old, her parents divorced, with her father leaving for California and her mother struggling to find steady work. Steinem saw her mother's inability to hold a job as evidence of discrimination against women—and those with mental illness—in the workplace.

After studying government at Smith College, Steinem began a career as a freelance writer. One of her first, and most famous, articles was an expose of New York City's Playboy Club she wrote for *Show* magazine. Steinem went undercover as a Playboy "bunny" to research her article, which exposed the sexism and exploitation the women at the club endured.

After freelancing for a few more years, she began writing regularly for *New York* magazine in 1968. What began as an insert in the magazine in December 1971 eventually became the feminist magazine *Ms.*, which Steinem spearheaded with Dorothy Pitman Hughes. The magazine was an immediate hit, with the first issue selling out in eight days. Steinem used the platform to discuss issues important to women, and the publication became the first national magazine to feature the subject of domestic violence on its cover.

(Left) Gloria Steinem, photographed by Lynn Gilbert in 1977

(Top right) Steinem speaking at the Women Together Arizona Summit in 2016, photo taken by Gage Skidmore

(Bottom right) Gloria Steinem shakes President Barack Obama's hand after receiving the Presidential Medal of Freedom in 2013.

Throughout the '70s and '80s, Steinem continued to write articles and essays exploring themes of feminism, and often lectured on a broad range of topics. Then, in 1986, she was diagnosed with breast cancer, which she fought with the same fierceness she brought to her work: She beat the cancer, celebrating her 84th birthday in 2018.

Although she saw the cancer as a sign she needed to "slow down," Steinem continues to stay active in feminist and social issues, and has won numerous awards and honors, including the 2013 Presidential Medal of Freedom and the Society of Professional Journalists' Lifetime Achievement Award.

Audre Lorde

The daughter of Caribbean immigrants, Audrey Geraldine Lorde was born on February 18, 1934 in New York City. A late bloomer, Lorde did not begin speaking until the age of four, and often had trouble communicating. But she took refuge in poetry—when her own words failed her, she would use poems to express her feelings.

By the time she was a teenager, she was writing poetry regularly. She went on to attend Hunter College and then Columbia University, where she earned a master's degree in library science in 1961. Her first book of poetry, *The First Cities*, was published in 1968. In her second book, *Cables to Rage*, which was published in 1970, Lorde addressed her own sexuality in the poem "Martha," in which she came out as a lesbian.

Lorde's works continued to explore issues of love, identity, and racial injustice, and 1976's *Coal* made her a leader in the Black Arts Movement. Her 1978 volume of poetry, *The Black Unicorn*, in which Lorde explored her own African heritage, is considered by many critics to be her most influential work.

Lorde continued to write even after being diagnosed with cancer in 1978, which she would fight for more than a decade. Her 1980 book *The Cancer Journals* documents her struggle with the disease.

(Left) A photo of Audre Lorde taken in 1980 in Austin, Texas

Lillian Smith

Lillian Eugenia Smith was born on December 12, 1897, in Jasper, Florida. After her father lost his job in 1915, the family moved to Clayton, Georgia. A lover of music, Smith studied at Piedmont College and the Peabody Conservatory before moving to China to direct music at a Methodist school for girls. Her time abroad opened her eyes to the oppression of Asians and African-Americans in her home country.

When Smith returned to Georgia, she became the head of the Laurel Falls Camp, a school which emphasized instruction in the arts and psychology. It was here that she met school counselor Paula Snelling, and the two maintained a closeted romantic relationship for the rest of their lives. Smith and Snelling created the literary magazine *Pseudopodia*, which often criticized the injustices of the racially segregated South and called for social reform.

In 1944, Smith published what would be her most famous work, the novel *Strange Fruit*. The book explored the theme of interracial romance and was so controversial that it was forbidden to mail it through the U.S. Postal Service.

Smith was unique as one of the first white women to vocally criticize racial injustice in the country. She would continue to support the civil rights movement until her death from cancer in 1966.

Toni Morrison

(Top left) President Barack Obama awards Toni Morrison with the Presidential Medal of Freedom at a White House ceremony in 2012.

Toni Morrison—born Chloe Ardelia Wofford on February 18, 1931, in Lorain, Ohio—grew up with parents who frequently told their children African American folktales and ghost stories. An avid reader, Morrison attended Howard University in Washington, D.C. and Cornell University in Ithaca, New York, where she earned a master's degree in English in 1955.

Morrison began her career as an English professor at Howard, but eventually moved to New York City to be a fiction editor for Random House, where she was the first black woman senior editor for the company. She began informally writing in the late '60s, when she would meet with a group of other poets and writers to discuss their work. It was during these meetings that she began developing her first novel, *The Bluest Eye*, which was published in 1970. The book did not sell well, but Morrison refused to be discouraged and continued to write.

Over the next few years, Morrison wrote books like *Sula*, which was nominated for a National Book Award, and *Song of Solomon*, which won a National Book Critics Circle Award. *Song of Solomon* put Morrison's name on the map, and became a favorite among readers.

Over the next decade, Morrison continued to write and teach; but her 1987 novel *Beloved* would change her life forever. The book is arguably her most celebrated work, winning the Pulitzer Prize for fiction and inspiring the Oscar-nominated film of the same name. Morrison went on to win the Nobel Prize in literature in 1993, becoming the first black woman—of any nationality—to win the award.

In addition to her novels, Morrison has branched out into other genres, writing several children's books—including *The Big Box* and *The Ant or the Grasshopper?*—and writing the lyrics for composer Andre Previn's *Four Songs* and for Richard Danielpour's *Sweet Talk*. She has also published nonfiction books, novellas, and even a modern opera libretto.

(Right) A photo of Toni Morrison at an autograph session at a bookstore in Paris, France, 2009

Pearl S. Buck

Born to Presbyterian missionaries on June 26, 1892, in Hillsboro, West Virginia, Pearl Comfort Sydenstricker spent the majority of her younger years in Zhenjiang, China. She attended boarding school in Shanghai in 1907, but was dismayed by some of the racist attitudes other students had towards the Chinese people. Pearl's parents had always emphasized that the people of China were their equals; this lesson would stick with her throughout her life.

Pearl returned to the U.S. to earn a philosophy degree at Randolph-Macon Woman's College in Virginia, then moved back to China to care for her ailing mother. There, she met and married missionary John Buck; although the pair would divorce in 1935, she would keep his name for the rest of her life.

In 1926, Pearl began writing in an attempt to support her parents, who were both in ill health. She published her first novel, *East Wind, West Wind*, in 1930, and her second, *The Good Earth*, in 1932. Both novels explored Chinese culture and traditions, with *The Good Earth* earning a Pulitzer Prize. In 1938, the writer became the first American woman to win the Nobel Prize in literature. On accepting the award, Pearl credited her beloved China for teaching her and inspiring her to write.

(Left) A photo of Pearl S. Buck from 1960. Buck died of lung cancer in 1973 at the age of 80.

0822